Curb and Leash Your Human

ANDREW LUDWIG AND RITA LUDWIG

authorHOUSE®

AuthorHouse™
1663 Liberty Drive
Bloomington, IN 47403
www.authorhouse.com
Phone: 1-800-839-8640

*Cover picture, from bottom to top: Lola (Micki's successor) with
her human; Osito and Koki with their human*

First published by AuthorHouse   7/21/2010

ISBN: 978-1-4520-5045-4 (e)
ISBN: 978-1-4520-5043-0 (sc)
ISBN: 978-1-4520-5044-7 (hc)

Library of Congress Control Number: 2010910031

Printed in the United States of America
Bloomington, Indiana

This book is printed on acid-free paper.

Dedicated to Andrew and Rita's dear friends
Micki, Koki and Osito

Foreword

This book is written by Andrew and Rita Ludwig. Both were beloved companions of author Luckii Ludwig. Andrew was the first, born in 1992. He started writing the book for dogs to explain how to live with crazy humans. He died in 2006 before he could finish the book.

Luckii was going to finish it for him, but before she got started, Rita appeared in her life. When Rita heard about the book, she decided to finish it because she didn't want any crazy human ideas in the book. After all, this was supposed to be a book for dogs.

Both dogs came into my life quite by accident. Andrew I met at a dog show in Davis, California, and I met Rita at a breeder's house in Carson City, Nevada. Both were whippets, which, if you are not familiar with them, look like small greyhounds. You'll see pictures of them in the book. Rita hired me to do the typing since she doesn't have thumbs and likes to save her energy for more important things.

Both look similar—white with brindle markings, but are as different as night and day, which is not surprising since one was male and one was female.

While I have my own recollections of meeting them both and the importance of them in my life, this is their book and their recollections about their lives, the humans in their lives and other important issues. I can only hope that somehow, I am as important to them as they are to me.

Koki and Osito Relaxing

Micki relaxing

Contents

Andrew - First Meeting

I WAS HEADED TO ANOTHER dog show; this time it was in Davis, California. I was born and lived in Concord, a mere hour away, so the ride wasn't going to be a long one.

My problem wasn't with the ride, because I loved riding in cars. My problem was that I had to share a kennel with my sister. I didn't like her too much; she was bossy and pushy. Needless to say, she didn't give me much room to spread my legs out. Mom had to go along also, because we were only three months old.

Our breeder was a nice enough woman, but she had too many dogs. Mom got to ride up front with her. Someday, I was going to ride in the front. None of us were allowed to put our heads out the window and feel the fresh air. We were told we could get hurt doing that. I never understood why we could get hurt. I thought air was soft and comforting.

Dog shows were not my favorite thing to do. I didn't know what my favorite thing to do was, but I knew there was something more fun out there than dog shows.

I'd only been in one show and I took second. I guess that would have been a big deal, except my sister took first, so, of course, she got all the praise and attention. Maybe that's why mom liked her best.

I didn't know much about humans and assumed you would always live with the one who brought you into the world. After all, I loved her and had no idea I could even love another human.

All of that changed the minute I spotted MY human walking onto the grounds of the park we were at. Oh, my goodness, I could tell just by looking at her that I wanted to live with her. She smelled like my soul-mate, even a hundred yards away.

We had just finished being shown and again, I took second to my sister, who was busy trying to lord it over me. I tried to ignore her and concentrate on my human.

She was with a friend and as they came closer, I could hear their conversation.

"So, how come you've never had a dog?" her friend asked.

She laughed; I loved her laugh.

"Oh, I don't know. Never had the time, I guess. All my friends have dogs, so I just enjoy them."

I knew I could make her forget all those other dogs, if she'd take me home with her.

"What kind would you have, if you had one?"

My ears perked up, waiting for the answer.

"A whippet," she replied quickly.

My heart started pounding and my body began to shake. I had to get her to notice me.

"A what?" her friend asked.

"A whippet—they are like greyhounds, only smaller."

We are not like greyhounds, I thought to myself. We're better.

When her friend asked why she wanted a whippet, she responded, "Some friends of mine had whippets and I just adored them. They were cute, affectionate and friendly, highly intelligent, too. They are elegant, funny and serious all at the same time. They are delightful."

I was ecstatic. This had to be my human, but how would I ever get her attention?

All of a sudden, her friend pointed towards us. "Look, whippets."

"Where?"

"Over in the corner; let's go."

My heart was in my throat as they approached. She was the most beautiful human I had ever seen. Well, okay, maybe not the most beautiful, but I knew I already loved her. The next thing I knew, they were standing next to my sister and my mom. Would she even notice me?

"How cute," my human observed. "How old are they?"

She glanced over at me. I know she did.

"Three months."

I almost gagged when she reached down to pet my sister, but, being the bitch she was, she snapped at my human. I could have killed her at that moment, but I was kind of glad she did it. My human looked at me. I so wanted to leap into her arms and beg her to take me home.

Our breeder explained that my sister didn't always take to strangers (excuse me, she never was nice to humans), but, she had taken first place in the dog show. She also noted the beautiful white and fawn coloring of her and her mom. Oh, barf!

She added that my sister and I had been in two shows, and, of course, had to mention I had placed second both times.

It was pointed out that I was white with dark brindle markings and had a spot on my side that looked like a saddle, and a cute exclamation mark on top of my head. I would have blushed if I knew what it all meant.

At that point, my human looked over at me and I sat up and stared right into her eyes.

"Are you interested in whippets?" my breeder asked.

"Well, actually, I've only met two and I absolutely loved them. I was telling my friend that if I ever got a dog, it would be a whippet."

"He is for sale," my breeder stated, and my hopes grew. "I'm keeping the female. I'd like to find a buyer for him soon. He's more than old enough to be on his own."

Way to go, breeder, I thought. Sell me to her.

My human muttered to her friend, "Sure he's expendable because he didn't come in first. Look at that face."

I tried to smile.

"But," the breeder interrupted, "you'd have to be willing to show him. He comes from good stock. His grandfather won several championships."

"Oh, I'm not into dog shows. I want a pet and companion, someone to go camping and fishing with."

Inside I was screaming—don't ruin it. I could see my breeder cringing at the thought of my doing something besides dog shows. But, I want to go; I'll do anything, even if I don't know how to fish or camp.

My breeder gave my human her card and mumbled something about calling her if she changed her mind.

What was I going to do? My human was getting away. Couldn't someone do something?

"You know, I could always show him for you," my breeder offered.

Say yes, say yes; anything to get me out of here and into your life.

"That would mean he'd be gone on weekends when I'm off work and would want him with me."

She's going to ruin it; say yes.

Her friend butted in, "Why would she want to show him if he always comes in second to his sister? You have a champion in her—why not let him go?"

Way to go friend, I cheered. Gang up on her and get me outta here.

"I'll have to think about that. I do need to find a home for him soon. Would you like to take him for a walk?"

This time, I could no longer sit still. I was up and running in circles. This was my chance. Take me for a walk and then we can sneak right on out of the park.

I knew all about how to please humans when you walk with them. I had been trained and knew what to do so I wouldn't get punished. I walked next to my human, sat when she stopped walking, and the whole time never took my eyes off her.

"Is that cute or what?" her friend commented. "He keeps looking up at you. You two are perfect together. He looks like he belongs to you."

I was beginning to like my human's friend; she might be the one to bring this whole thing together. I decided to be nice to her, too.

Several people stopped and commented on how cute I was. I was getting a lot of help.

"What's his name?" someone asked.

"Actually, I don't know. He's really not mine—yet."

Oh my God, she said yet. How can I keep cool when I know she's considering taking me home with her? Oh my God, oh my God, this might really happen.

When we returned, I went to my bed and sat patiently, looking at my human.

"What's his name?" my human asked.

The breeder pulled out all my papers with a long list of pedigrees and stuff. I knew my human would not care about any of it; she just wanted me.

"We call him Hit Man. I'm a big basketball fan and all the pups in his litter were given nicknames of the players on the US Olympic team."

"So, he was named after Charles Barkley?"

"You're a fan, too. Yes, he was named after Charles."

Way to go, human. You are scoring points with my breeder. Keep it up and I'll win this game.

"He doesn't look like a Hit Man to me," my human said as she stared into my very soul. I stared right back.

"Oh, he isn't, but none of the guys were nicknamed Marshmallow. Tell you what; I really want to find a home for him soon. Give me your phone number and if I can't place him with someone who will show him, I'll call and see if you are still interested.

My human leaned down and hugged me. The world stood still. "Oh, I'll still be interested," she replied.

She looked sad as she turned to leave, and I was too. But, I had high hopes. I knew she knew we were meant for each other. I was going to do everything and anything I had to so no one else would want me. My breeder was going to be making that call soon.

I was miserable at home. I didn't want my human to forget me, and I didn't want my breeder to sell me to someone else. I fought with my sister and mom. I knocked over all the water dishes as soon as the breeder filled them. I didn't care if they were upset with me.

What I didn't know was that my human's friend called the breeder and convinced her somehow that my human was perfect for me. I'll always be grateful to that friend. In the meantime, I continued to misbehave and knew my breeder would give me up eventually.

I was lying outside in the sun one afternoon and I swore I heard my human's voice. I thought I must be dreaming, but I knew that voice. I jumped up and ran inside. I scurried around the corner, slid on the rug and came to a stop at my human's feet. It was a dream comes true.

My breeder laughed, "I'd say he remembers you."

No kidding, I remembered. All my work had paid off and she was here to take me home with her.

Apparently, they had paper work to do and the breeder explained about the special leashes she used for us so we wouldn't hurt our necks if we lunged at something and she gave my leash to my human. She also said to never let me off leash because I loved to run and would run away from her.

I was never going to leave my human.

The breeder also told her to put up or hide garbage and trash cans because whippets were garbage hounds. Darn, I wished she hadn't told her that. And, she said, I needed a kennel to sleep in or I'd be under the covers all night. I was pretty sure my human would want me there; I could tell.

They were taking too much time for instructions. I wanted to get out of there. But, no, I had to have my last shot and a bath. My human went with me and we never let each other out of our sight. I whimpered when I got my shot. The breeder said I always did that even though it didn't hurt.

Finally, I was ready to go. The breeder slipped my collar on me and handed the leash to my human and we smiled at each other. We walked out the door and I never looked back.

Rita - First Meeting

I WAS BORN IN 2003 into the Cove Creek Whippets family. I was, of course, the most beautiful and intelligent of the litter. My mother, Helen, treated me as though I were more special than the others.

Oh, I know, mothers aren't supposed to have favorites, but I was that exceptional. I think she liked my sister, Anna, so the two of us became close friends.

Dennis was in charge of the breeding and training. I was considered one of the best for dog shows. He was such a pushover. All I had to do was rest my chin on his knee and bat my big brown eyes at him, and I got everything I wanted.

When we were old enough, we went to live with Karen, the other kennel owner. We became like her children and had lots of freedom. She was kind and gentle with us and tolerant of most of the things puppies do, but she was not the pushover Dennis was.

We got to run through the house and play. When we needed to go outside to do our business, we did. She didn't have to come out and check on us to make sure we were behaving. Most of us didn't enjoy digging, so that wasn't a problem.

One day, I was bored, so I jumped the fence to see what was on the other side. I needed a little more excitement in my life, and it was exciting out in the world. We lived near a golf course and I found all kinds of things to chase, like little four-legged creatures that could run fast, so I chased them.

But, somewhere along the route, I got lost and hadn't paid attention to where I was in relationship to my house. It got dark and I wanted to be home where it was warm and I could get something to eat. I finally found a place to hide and laid down for a nap. I was tired and scared. There were all kinds of strange noises out there that I'd never heard before. I knew I would have to find my way home the next day.

I'm not sure how many days I was lost, but I was plenty worried about getting back home. The nights were the worst because I didn't know what to expect or what I might run into. As I was wandering, I found a road and stopped running for a while. I didn't know if the road would take me home or not, so I just sat there, contemplating what to do.

All of a sudden, I heard Karen's voice calling my name, but I couldn't see her. I sat up and there she was. I ran to her and gave her a kiss; she was so happy to see me. I'm not usually free with my kisses unless it is somehow going to benefit me. She picked me up and took me home. I was never allowed to go out in the back yard by myself again.

They started taking me lots of places and showed me to other people. They said I was winning points, but I never saw any points so they meant nothing to me. My breeders got a great deal of pleasure out of those stupid points, and I got extra treats.

I got my championship papers within a year from the American Kennel Club. I couldn't believe someone actually issues a paper for that sort of thing. All along, I thought papers were issued to dogs to assist in potty training.

So, done with being a champion, now I was going to have some fun. People always pick out some good looking male for you to have fun with. But, if you can't stand him, they will find someone else. The only thing about having fun is, of course, you have to give birth to the pups, so I did-- all eight of them.

They were kind of cute and since they couldn't see when they were born, it was pretty easy to take care of them. When I got tired of them, I would slip away and not have to worry; they didn't know what I looked like.

Okay, so laugh—it was worth a shot. We all know our own by how we smell and a few other factors I won't get into. Funny, I don't recall seeing humans smell each other. Since we know that humans are not exactly discreet, they must have some other way to identify their own, or maybe they don't care to identify them.

Of course, human children live with their parents forever, at least one hundred years or more (in our years).

I guess if you hang out with anyone that long, you'd start to recognize them. Whippets all have their own distinct markings, so once you meet someone, you can tell who they are by how they look. I don't think humans can do that—they all look alike.

After my first litter, I got to return to my beauty queen style of life. I was gorgeous, was a champion, and gave my people some beautiful pups, which, thank God, they found good homes for.

Then there was this thing about shows. I was supposed to do what? Hadn't I given my all? They wanted me to parade around with a bunch of psychologically challenged mutts who thought they were better than me? But, the kicker was, one of us was going to be picked as best in show! What the hell does that mean? It means nothing to a dog.

To add insult to injury, the best in show was going to be picked by a human! Oh, please, what do they really know about us? They've never been in our paws. I can name at least a dozen dogs (all related to me) that would make better judges.

I went to work on my breeders to see if I could just go and have some more fun. This time, they selected the guy I would have picked in the first place, Timmy. Was he handsome? He was like THE dog of all dogs. I started to say he was the God of all dogs, but I remembered humans use that term for someone really special to them. I still think one of them was dyslexic and got the spelling wrong, so I don't want to make that same mistake.

Timmy and I had a ball. Poor Timmy was pooped when I finally let him go.

I had eight pups the first time around, which I guess is pretty normal. The second batch started coming and after eight, everyone thought I was through. I wished I were through; it's hard work. But, I knew there was one left and he didn't seem to want to come out.

Dennis and Karen knew I was still in labor and struggling, so they put me in a box and headed to the vet. By the time we arrived, Ivan had been born and I was busy cleaning him. Isn't that just like a kid to make his mother suffer a little longer?

That was it for having fun and giving birth. I guess seventeen was enough for Dennis and Karen. Timmy and I continued to live together, but I didn't get to stay home and return to my beauty queen style of living. It was time to do that damn show thing again.

Even though I couldn't talk, I let them know that I wasn't interested in doing any more shows. My sister, Anna, loved the spotlight; let her do the shows. I wanted to hang out at home with Timmy, go on outings to Lake Tahoe and other fun places. Maybe Karen would even let me take over running her life.

Timmy said if I didn't do what the breeders wanted, they would sell me to some stranger just like they did with the pups. What did he know? He was a stupid male. He said he had heard them talking about finding a home for me. I told him he was crazy; I had a perfectly good home.

He said some old lady had told them she was looking for an adult whippet because her other dog had died. Well, I knew they weren't talking about me.

One day, a woman came to visit. I'd never seen her in my life. Karen introduced me to her. Why me? Timmy and my few remaining pups were put in another room, and suddenly, I knew what Timmy had been talking about. Oh, she was nice enough and had some great jerky treats in her pocket that she willingly shared with me, but I wasn't going anywhere with her.

Dennis filed my nails and showed this human how to do it. They talked a lot about me and what I was like. I began to panic. She wanted me to go with her. They signed some papers and gave her my collar and leash. Before I knew it, I was in her truck heading down the road, away from my home.

I was nervous and apprehensive. I whined and paced from the front seat to the back seat. She wanted me to settle down. How did she expect me to do that? Was I really going to live with someone else? Maybe this was temporary. Maybe she was going to try and teach me to like dog shows.

She talked to me the entire ride. I didn't want to listen. I had just been kidnapped from my home. Nothing she said could reassure me. Nothing she said was important to me. Did she expect me to change my whole life in one fell swoop?

We arrived at her place and she said this was going to be my new home. What the hell? It didn't look anything like Karen's house or Dennis' for that matter. None of the smells were familiar.

I wandered around; checking it all out, but I didn't like any of it. She showed me where my kennel was; I could tell it had belonged to some other dog. There was a bed on the floor which I assumed was for me since there were no other dogs in the house. It smelled new.

She said I could sleep with her, but I couldn't sleep. I sat on the end of her bed, keeping alert to every new sound and movement. When would the nightmare be over?

There was a cat named Charlie living here, too. I knew I didn't like that. She said he was mostly an outdoor cat and not to worry about him. Did she think I'd worry about some dumb cat? He took one look at me and split. He knew better than to mess with me.

I kept thinking about what Timmy had said. I hoped he was wrong and that someone would come and take me home tomorrow or the next day.

I finally crawled onto the dog bed, but I still couldn't sleep. I dozed for a while, but every noise had me up and pacing through the house. Nothing was the same and there was nothing that made me feel safe.

If someone didn't come and get me, maybe I'd have to escape and find my way back home. But, we had driven for hours and I never paid attention to the route.

I wondered if my breeders knew I had been kidnapped. Of course they did; they signed me over to this human. What were they thinking?

Finally, I crawled onto the human's bed. She was awake, too, and held me close to her. It didn't make me feel any better, but I was able to sleep.

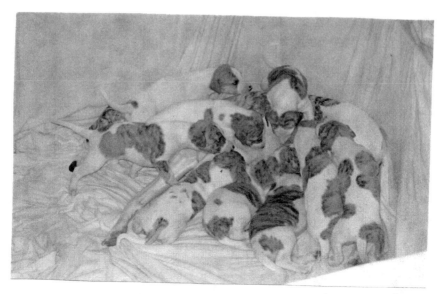

Rita and her second litter—all nine of them

Andrew - First Weeks

THE RIDE TO MY HUMAN's home was exciting. I was going to be with her forever. I had hoped she would let me sit up front with her, but maybe she would the next time. Maybe she'd even let me hang my head out the window, but if she didn't, I'd still go anywhere with her.

She told me my new name would be Andrew. I liked that; I didn't like being called Hit Man. Andrew, I found out, was the name she would have given her son, if she'd had one. Guess I was going to have the same status of a son. Also, there was a saint named Andrew, but I never knew him, and there was a golf course somewhere in Scotland named Andrew. I suppose that was important. None of that mattered; I liked the name.

When we arrived at my new home, I could hardly contain myself. It would be a place of my own to share with my human who rescued me. I followed her to the door, anxious to start my new life.

The first thing I saw as we entered was this big furry thing sitting on the end of the kitchen counter, staring at me. It was a cat and I'd never seen one before. I was intrigued.

Her name was Susan and her look told me everything I needed to know. It was her house and she would share it with me if I did everything I was told. If she gave me her "evil eye" look, it would be a warning, but if she gave me the two "evil eye" look, I was in trouble. I knew I'd learn how to get along with her real fast.

My human took me on a tour of my new surroundings. Susan jumped down and followed us, so I was on my best behavior. I kept one eye on her and one on my human. When my human showed me where my food and water dish were located, I realized I was hungry. She gave me some food. Susan walked over to it, smelled it, turned and opened her mouth as though she was going to hiss, but no sound came out. I decided to eat when she wasn't watching.

My kennel was taken out of the car and placed on the floor right next to my human's bed. Susan looked in, made a face with her mouth open and walked away. Whew! At least she wasn't going to share my kennel. My human even told her she was not allowed inside. I think she got the message.

We went for a walk and I was shown where I could do my business. There were a lot of grassy areas, but no fences. I decided not to use the grass next to our house and went to the neighbor's yard to relieve myself. My human didn't seem to mind and cleaned up after me.

While we were there, she decided to take me in to meet the neighbor. I was hoping she wouldn't tell her I had just pooped on her lawn.

"Hi, Nellie. This is Andrew, my new dog." She sat on the couch, so I climbed up next to her.

"How old is he?"

"Three months."

"Oh, boy—a whirling dervish!"

As long as I knew Nellie, she always brought up that whirling dervish thing because she was surprised I wasn't like that. I never knew what a whirling dervish was. It must be a human thing.

That first night, I was put to bed in my kennel, but my human didn't shut the door, so in the middle of the night, I jumped up on her bed. To my surprise, she lifted the covers and let me under. Ahh, we had flannel sheets; what a luxury. I was in heaven and slept with her every night after that.

When I wanted peace and quiet, I went to my kennel. It became a haven for me and Susan was not allowed inside.

I had a nice water dish next to my food dish, but I discovered it was easier and more fun to drink from the toilet. My human let me do it because she knew I'd always have access to nice, cold, fresh water. She also let me lick the water off her legs when she got out of the shower. That was lots of fun.

Susan did her best to try and run my life. She thought I was a patsy just waiting to be had, by her. She discovered early on that I was attracted to what I call "kitty rocka". It wasn't that I was so attracted; I was surprised she had a place indoors to do her business and I wanted to see what she'd done.

Every time she'd get in that box and start scratching around, I'd run to see what she was doing. My human would come running too and remove Susan's stuff before I could get a look at it. It kind of became a game we all played. Susan seemed disappointed that I didn't get in trouble.

One day, our human put an empty box on the end of the counter. She said she was going to recycle it, but Susan had different ideas. She would climb in the box and start scratching and I would immediately come running.

She'd wait until I saw her in that box and then duck down so I couldn't see her. I knew I'd been had, so I would bark at her. I could hear her giggling in the box. Our human was amused by all this, so she left the box on the counter and every evening, Susan would play her little trick on me.

Finally, I decided to fight back. Two could play this game, I thought. She scratched, I ran. She ducked and I barked. However, it didn't stop there. I quietly hid under the end of the counter where she couldn't see me. Susan couldn't stand not knowing what I was up to, so she stood up and peered over the side of the box. I leaped out and barked at her. She dived back into the box and I went back under the counter. It was such a fun game and totally entertaining for our human.

Susan would eventually emerge and declare she was the winner, sauntering across the counter top, daring me to try and get her.

The box eventually disappeared and I was convinced Susan wanted to play with me. I had this rope-a-dope toy I enjoyed, so I would drag it through the house, tossing it in the air near Susan. She always positioned herself in my path.

However, that's all she did—just sat there and watched like I was supposed to entertain her. One time, I came so close; she actually reached out, touched the rope and yawned. That was the extent of her playing.

My human tried to teach me a game she called fetch. What a stupid game. She threw a tennis ball and being the obedient dog that I was, I ran, retrieved it and brought it back to her. She threw it away again. What the hell was that all about? Why should I go and get it again if she really didn't want it?

I did think Susan might like to play catch with me. I'd sit about five feet from her and nudge the ball towards her, but she sat there like a statue and never nudged it back. I'd go get the ball and try again, but she never even looked at the ball. She wasn't very athletic.

One time, though, the ball hit her paw and she moved it away. I jumped in the air and ran around in circles. She was playing with me. Susan was amused, stood, stretched and smiled as she walked away. Her new puppy had been had again.

My human took me everywhere with her, except for the times she'd sneak out and do something without me. I loved it and I always got to ride shotgun. She never did roll down that window, so I never got to feel the air in my face.

We'd go to her friends' houses and they always said I was welcome and that I was better behaved than she was. Actually, I didn't know what to do around those strange people and I didn't want my human to leave me there, so I'd sit quietly by her side and watch.

We had to go to obedience school. Like I needed to learn any more than I already knew? I'd been through all that stuff, but my human said she needed to learn how to communicate with me. She wanted to be able to let me off leash sometimes and be able to let me know what was okay for me to do.

I carefully watched the other dogs to see what they did wrong, because when they did something wrong, their humans would yank on the chains around their necks. I flinched every time one of them got jerked around. When it was my turn, I made sure I didn't do anything to cause my human to jerk my chain.

The instructor thought I needed to know the feeling of the chain. I didn't think so. When my human refused to trick me into doing something wrong, the instructor took me, tricked me into making a mistake and yanked my chain. I never forgave her for that and when I saw her years later, I ran behind my human and hid.

We graduated from the stupid school, but I wasn't tops in my class because when we did the "down" thing, I would go down, but not so my belly rested on the cold, hard concrete. I could stay like that forever with my belly hovering over the ground, until my human released me.

I know my human understood about the down thing because she never made me do it. If she wanted me to stay, I stayed, sitting upright.

She did pretty well at learning how to communicate with me, but her communication skills were primitive. We both knew that I knew more than she did. I always behaved the way I thought she wanted me to and let her think she was the one getting me to do it her way. She was easy to work with and so easy to control.

One night, I went to bed early. She was watching a PBS show about how to tell if your dog is intelligent. Geeze, she could have asked me. There were three dogs on the show—a basenji, lab and basset hound.

They placed two bricks on the floor with a 4x6 board over them. Each dog's favorite treat was placed under the board.

The basenji circled the board twice, knelt down and scooped the treat out. The lab ran around the board several times and then tore the board from off the bricks and ate the treat. The basset is still sitting by the board wondering what to do.

My human set up the same experiment in the living room. She woke me from a sound sleep and led me to the living room. I immediately smelled the chicken, walked over to the board, knelt down and scooped up the chicken and went back to bed. What a genius!

The laundry room was doggie prison. If I did anything wrong, I was locked up in that room and told to think about what I did. What did that mean? Most of the time, I didn't even realize I had done anything wrong, like the time I found a pen on the floor. Chewed on it and got ink on the rug. Like, what was wrong with that? If my human didn't want ink on the rug, why did she leave a pen on the floor?

It didn't take long to figure out that there were some things I didn't think were wrong, but my human did. We had been sleeping for months with flannel sheets on the bed and suddenly, they disappeared. I knew my human had taken them off and washed them, but now, we had different kinds of sheets and they weren't as soft.

I knew she kept the sheets in a closet in the bathroom, so I went and opened the door. Sure enough, there they were on a shelf right in front of my face. I pulled one out and the second it hit the floor, I knew I was going to be in big trouble. I didn't know how to put it back. My whole day was ruined.

When my human came home, I quietly slinked right past her and went into the laundry room. She knew I'd done something wrong and said, "You go in there, young man, and think about what you did." What was there to think about? I'd been thinking all day and never came up with an answer. I knew she was going to take me back to the breeder. It would break my heart.

Finally, after what seemed an eternity, she opened the door, bent down and gave me a hug. Maybe she wasn't too mad at me.

"Okay, follow me," she directed. I didn't want to go because I knew we were headed for the bathroom. I moved slowly with my head bent down.

She sat on the floor next the sheet I'd pulled out. "Did you do this?" she asked.

I turned my head; I couldn't look at her.

"Sweetie," she began, "it's too hot for flannel sheets. We have to put them away for the summer, but as soon as it starts to get cold, we'll put them back on the bed."

She pulled me closer to her and hugged and kissed me. I kissed her back. I knew she forgave me. I never did that again. In the fall, the flannel sheets came out again and I circled the bed, excited and happy.

Andrew and Susan sharing time together

Rita - First Weeks

I KNEW I WOULDN'T BE in this human's life for long. Someone would come and get me, or she'd get tired of me and take me home. At any rate, I decided not to get too excited about anything.

My first day, we went for several walks. I was nervous because there were all kinds of new noises I'd never heard before. That first morning, we walked for miles. It felt good to get out and go some place, even though I didn't know where we were.

She talked to me the whole time. It was so annoying. I was trying to ignore her. You'd think she'd have the good sense to do the same. We kept running into people who knew her and they always wanted to stop and pet me.

For Pete's sake, I was just here visiting. This human was not going to change my entire life. At least she kept calling me Rita.

At one point, I heard a lot of loud noises. There were some strange men in a truck pointing and yelling at me. I bolted and pulled the leash right out of my human's hands. I ran away as fast as I could, but I had no idea where I was going.

Nothing looked familiar and I was certain my home wasn't anywhere near where I was, but I kept running. Soon, I was tired. I think I managed to lose my leash. I ended up on a porch somewhere. A nice woman was sitting there and she let me sit down to rest. I wanted to go home.

Suddenly, a car pulled up and the human who had snatched me from my home, jumped out. She was crying and looking up towards the sky. She came up on the porch and hugged me. I guess I was glad to see her because she was the only familiar thing around me. There was another car with people who came up on the porch also, and that truck with the strange men in it, showed up too.

They were all talking at the same time, telling the woman on the porch how they all lived in the senior mobile home park around the corner. Somehow, the human who snatched me, had been able to mobilize all those old farts into looking for me. Dogs seem to be important to these people. Besides, they are all retired and had nothing better to do than look for a dog.

In a way, I was flattered to think I was so important to all those people who didn't even know me. Maybe they did it because my human was important to them. Whatever the reason, I was happy they found me; the thought of spending a night lost and cold terrified me.

We went home and she gave me a couple of treats. She didn't seem angry or anything. She said she was so happy I was home. I went in and rested on her pillow while I thought things over. I put my chin on the window sill. It was an easy thing to do and I could look out and watch everyone go by.

I finally came to the realization that perhaps I was going to be here a lot longer than I had anticipated. If that were the case, I better settle down and figure out how I was going to take control of the situation. This human did seem to genuinely like me.

But, after all, there were two of us bitches living in this house, and by God, I was going to be the head bitch.

My human tried to console me and explain our living situation and how things were going to be. I knew I had to take charge, soon. One more day of her ideas and I might never gain control.

People stopped by and called to see if I'd been found. Apparently that was the big excitement for the day in the senior's park. Well, that and when the meat wagon came. That's what they call the ambulance which they say comes in here a lot. They all want to know who is being taken out.

I heard a couple of them talking and they call this place the Bermuda Triangle because they live here, then the meat wagon comes and takes them to a convalescent hospital a block away and after that, they go across the street to the cemetery. They all laugh about it, but I don't get it.

Late in the afternoon, a strange man walked into our house. He greeted me, put his hand out so I could smell it and sat down on the floor. He seemed nice, was very quiet and offered me a treat. That was the least he could do. He didn't stay long.

Every day for a week, he would stop by and sit on the floor with me. He was always calm and always brought me a treat. I started to like him, a little. He told me he had two dogs and showed me pictures of them. I guess he thought I cared about Shiba Inus. I'd never heard of them. He said someday I could meet them and maybe we could all go for a walk. I hadn't even thought about doing that. Why do humans always think they should be the ones in charge?

One day, we went to a place I came to know as the overcrossing. Humans are so funny; they name places that have no real names. There's an empty field somewhere; it doesn't have a name, but humans call it the field of dreams because it's loaded with rabbits. You walk through an area with lots of trees; it doesn't have a name, but humans call it the green belt. And, there's the arboretum, the Road 102 slough, the duck pond; they name everything. It does help me know where I'm being taken; I've learned all the names and I loved going to the overcrossing. It was a wonderful place.

It was a tree-lined road out in the middle of nowhere. There were a few buildings near it, but you could barely see them through the trees. There were tons of squirrels running all around. I'd never seen so many at one time.

To my surprise, I was let off the leash and told to keep my human in my sight at all times. I took off after the squirrels and had the time of my life. I wore myself out trying to catch one, but they would always run up a tree or dive back into the holes they had dug.

I tried digging them out, but that was too much work and I knew I'd never get deep enough to catch one. I had to develop a new method of capturing them. One time, I even tried to climb a tree after a squirrel. Getting down was the hard part.

Going to the overcrossing became a daily event. I always knew when we made a certain turn in the road where we were going. I would sit up in the seat and start searching for the critters. I would get so excited; I would shake all over in anticipation.

David, the man who always came to see me, showed up one day with his two dogs. I wasn't sure about them or about sharing my squirrel hunting grounds with them.

Osito was very nice and friendly and came over to meet me. We touched noses and then she went to my human for a treat. I had never realized she always had treats with her, so I got one, too. I think the only reason Osito was there was for the treats. Osito was always looking for something to eat. I noticed she often stopped and ate what looked like squirrel poop. David would tell her to stop, but she never did.

Koki was standoffish and didn't seem to care for me, but that was okay because I didn't like her too much either. We mostly ignored each other.

David did not let his girls off leash, so I got to do the entire squirrel chasing. Koki would get excited and looked like she wanted in on the fun, so one day David let her off the leash. She didn't have the first idea of how to chase squirrels, so I had to show her.

I had come up with a new strategy for how to catch squirrels, but I needed a partner to accomplish it. Koki and I formed an unspoken plan on how to hunt.

When we'd see a squirrel run into a bush, we'd charge the bush. Koki's job was to run around the bush as fast as she could. She was also supposed to go through the bush, on top of the bush, or wherever I wanted her to go, and she'd do it.

I, on the other hand, would figure out where I thought the squirrel would exit from the bush and I would sit and wait for Koki to flush it out. Most of the time, the squirrel never came out.

My plan worked one day. Koki wore herself out going through the bush and the squirrel exited right where I thought it would and I nailed it. I was ready to move on to the next squirrel, but they wanted to play with it. Osito wanted to eat it and take it home. How gross!

Koki and I worked several techniques for catching squirrels, but they were hard to catch, so we graduated to rabbits. The large empty field near the overcrossing had lots of rabbits. They were much more fun to chase because they ran for long distances and did not climb trees.

Some days, we were so tired from chasing rabbits, we could barely make it back to the car. We'd drink some water and sit on the grass, panting and tired.

Soon, we were all traveling together to new and exciting places. Whenever we rode in my car, I would sit up front and David and his girls would sit in the back. When we rode with David, I would sit up front and my human would sit in the back with his girls. I always gave David a kiss when I jumped in the car because he knew who was in charge. My human was beginning to realize that also.

One afternoon, we were chasing rabbits at the overcrossing. I hadn't felt good all day, but as soon as I saw a rabbit, I forgot about how I felt.

When we came back for some water, my human told David she thought there was something wrong with me. She didn't know what it was, but she knew I didn't feel good.

The next morning she called the vet. I had met this woman once before when I went in for a checkup and to get on their list of future victims. By the time we got there, I really didn't feel good. There was some talk about a possible urinary infection.

They took me in the back so I could give them a urine sample and I never saw my human again. What was going on? Where did my human go? They said I had to have an emergency hysterectomy because my uterus was full of poisonous toxins and I would die if I didn't have the surgery.

I don't remember anything after that. I guess I went to sleep. When I woke up, I was tired and sore. I had stitches in my belly. Where was my human and what had they done to her? I wanted to go home.

My human rescued me later that day. They told her she had saved my life and were surprised my uterus hadn't broken the day before when I was chasing rabbits. Darn, now I was going to owe her for saving my life?

I had to take these horrible pills which my human tried to hide in chicken or peanut butter. I knew they were there, but I humored her by taking them because, after all, she had saved my life. And, it was a life I was beginning to enjoy. Plus, I didn't often get peanut butter.

The restrictions on chasing squirrels and rabbits were unbearable. I never got to go anywhere I could run. It seemed like an eternity. Every place we went with David, Koki and Osito, we all had to be on leashes. If she did let me off leash, we were at a place where there was nothing to chase. It was so boring.

We drove past the road leading to the overcrossing one afternoon, but she didn't turn; she kept going. I turned and stared at her and let out a big sigh. She pretended not to notice, so I started curling my lip up at her. Again, no response, so I let out one loud, sharp, shill bark, but it didn't help.

Soon the whole ordeal was over and things went back to normal.

We took a lot of walks every day and I met a lot of her friends and people who lived in the park. Many of them had dogs, which I could take or leave, but when we saw them, the dogs and I always got treats.

I met the dog who lived across the street. Her name was Micki. She and Koki and Osito had all known Andrew and they all liked him. I wasn't sure any of them liked me, but I didn't care.

Micki was a slightly overweight minpin who didn't chase anything, except maybe cats. I wasn't supposed to chase any cats that had names or were living in houses where we visited. I think Charlie had something to do with that.

Anyway, Micki liked my human a lot. Of course, she always had treats. As much as we all like treats, humans need to know that we can't always be bought off with them. Well, okay, maybe we can, but we don't have to lose our control over them because of it.

I used to get ice cubes at Micki's house. I love chewing on them and humans love to watch me do it. I make ice cubes sound so good you'd think I was eating filet mignon.

Let me tell you something about ice cubes. The best ones are not the ones that come out of the freezer. The best ones are the ones that come directly out of a human's glass, especially if they are drinking a margarita or a vodka tonic.

Since I was beginning to like my new life and was considering hanging around for a while, I decided I needed to learn how to control my human. Obviously, she hadn't learned anything from Andrew about who was in control. He was a mama's boy and probably did everything he could to please her.

I'm not so easy. I like things my way and needed to refine my techniques so she wouldn't know that she wasn't in charge. Her friends and neighbors knew I was the one in charge. In fact, they started calling me "Rita In Charge."

When it was announced that the park we lived in was getting a new manager, people would stop us and ask if I was going to be the new manager. I was, of course, flattered, but really, I don't have to work for a living; I'm well taken care of. Come to think of it, I don't remember my human doing much work either.

It didn't take long to have her under my paw. She liked me more than I liked her, so she was much more willing to please me than I was her. I think she still felt guilty about kidnapping me from a home—a home that was becoming a faint memory.

Oh, don't get me wrong, I did my part sometimes. I always pretended to listen when she talked to me, and she was always talking, except when I was asleep.

I never complained when she went golfing, as long as she took me out hunting before and after she played golf. I didn't laugh or get embarrassed no matter what she wore. I cleaned her hands every night before we went to bed. And, probably the most important thing of all, I always did the things she wanted me to, if I thought they would help me keep control.

Rita climbing a tree

Andrew – Spirits

ALL CREATURES ARE BORN WITH spirits who guide and protect them throughout their lives. Not everyone is aware of this. Animals and humans alike have these spirits, even if they choose not to recognize or call on them. But, none of us is so great, so perfect or so independent that we can make it on our own. We all need some help to get through this world.

Some people have more than one spirit to guide them. I think it's because people really need a lot of help to get through life. As far as I can tell, dogs only have one spirit—that's all we need.

I met my spirit when I was still very young. He came to me after I had taken second place in my first dog show. I was discouraged and down-hearted. He was consoling and promised he would find something better for me. It was easy for me to trust my spirit and listen to what he had to say. Unlike humans, dogs instinctively know they have a spirit and have no ego problems to get in the way of following what the spirit tells you.

He did warn me, however, that when the time came, I would have to agree to a contract with him as to my purpose in life and I would have to keep my promise. I wasn't sure what he meant by that, but I kept my eyes and ears open.

When my spirit was ready, he came to me and told me the contract I would have to agree to had been prepared and did I want to know what it was. Of course, I wanted to know. I didn't want to wander around the rest of whatever not knowing why I was here.

He said he would find the perfect human for me to be with and my purpose in life was to love her, protect her and teach her about unconditional love because she had never had any in her life.

I loved it and agreed to the contract with my spirit. He said he would always be there for me and would help me fulfill my purpose. Whenever I needed help, I could call on him.

That was all well and good, but I still didn't know what he was talking about, until that day at my second dog show. My spirit was there and even told me I would take second place again to my sister. He said it was necessary in order for my human to have the chance to have me in her life.

He explained that he had been working with the spirit of a human who would be at the show and we would know we were meant for each other. He said I would be like a son to her and she would be like a mother to me. That's exactly what happened.

It was easy to love my mom and easy to show her unconditional love. I wasn't sure how I could protect her. She seemed to be able to take care of herself without my help.

One morning, we took an early walk towards town. It was still a little dark out, but we knew where we were going.

Suddenly, some crazy man came towards us, ranting and raving about something. Mom tensed up and tightened up on my leash. I could sense she was afraid, so I started growling and looking mean.

The man came closer and shouted some nasty names at us and began taunting me. I was nervous, but my spirit was with me and reassured me that we would be alright and I'd know what to do when the time came.

Mom warned the man that I was attack trained and if he came one step closer, she would release me. He laughed at us and pointed at me. I looked to my spirit and asked what attack trained meant. He smiled and told me not to worry.

Well, the man stepped closer, lunging towards me while I barked my head off.

"What's he going to do? Piss on my leg?" the man laughed. Then, he called her some horrible names. She reached down and took off my leash. As I lunged for him, he turned to run and I bit him in the ass.

"Your damn dog better be vaccinated," he screamed. "I'll sue you."

"You better be vaccinated also," she retorted. "If anything happens to my dog, I'll kill you.""

He ran away and we both breathed a sigh of relief. She bent down and kissed me. "Thanks for protecting me, Andrew. You are a brave dog."

I kissed her back and looked for my spirit. "Thank you," I whispered to him.

I knew I could protect her. I was living up to the contract I had made with my spirit.

There was one more time when I had to protect her, and again, without my spirit to guide me, I would have been helpless.

We used to go fishing, camping and hiking at this lake we both loved. She used to tell me that when we both died, we would be cremated and our ashes would be scattered over the lake where we would rest in peace together, for eternity. I had no idea what she was talking about, but I got the part that we would always be together and I liked that idea.

During one of our hikes on this hill we often went to, we went a new direction down one of the paths. She liked this hill because she could look and see for miles around us. She often said if she won the lottery, she was going to build a nine hole golf course up there.

As we walked along, mom stopped suddenly and froze. I looked at her and knew something was wrong. There was something ahead of us on the trail that made her nervous.

She whispered to me that we had to go back and do it quietly. I still didn't know what was bothering her, so I looked down the path. There was a brown fuzzy thing sitting in the way. I didn't know what it was, but it was frightening my mom, so I started barking and running towards it.

"No, no, Andrew, come back," she yelled, but I kept going.

I was almost to the brown creature when it stood up. I froze. It was huge. I didn't know it was a bear; I'd never seen one before. I was beginning to understand why mom wanted us to go back. It was too late now.

Since I'd never encountered a bear before, I didn't know what to do. Every hair on my body was standing straight up and that's kind of hard to do because I have real short hair.

I started barking and running in circles around the bear. He would turn and try to keep up with me, but I was so much faster. Finally, he became so annoyed, he turned and ran away. I looked up and my spirit smiled at me. Whew!

My human was crying when I returned to her, and she held me close. She was thanking her spirits too. We never went down that trail again.

While I only have one spirit, my mom has several. She says she can't see her spirits, but I can. Well, at least I can see two of them. She may have more, but they haven't made themselves known to me. One of them is a short, funny guy. He laughs a lot and often pulls funny jokes on her. I know this because sometimes I hear her yell at him telling him it's not funny what he did.

The other spirit I see is a tall, slender woman with long hair. She looks more like an angel than a spirit. She is kind and gentle. My spirit seems to know her too, so she must be the one he worked with to get me together with my human.

The dogs I know have a spirit and I have only met a few who refuse to acknowledge their existence; they lead a pretty miserable life. They are not happy, they misbehave and I'm sure they never agreed to a contract with their spirit and if they did, they certainly didn't honor their contract.

Humans are no different; many do not acknowledge their spirits. For humans, I think their egos get in the way of accepting help. For some, learning why they are here and what their purpose is in life isn't important. Very few know they made a contract with their spirits early on.

The humans who can see their spirits are blessed because their spirits are always there and offer continual guidance. Some humans can see their spirits and the spirits of others. They are not crazy like some think; they have special gifts and are here to help others.

Even though my mom says she can't see her spirits, I know it is comforting for her to know they are there to help her through life. I hear her talking to them every morning when we go for a walk. She calls on them for help, guidance, strength and good health all the time.

Mom even swears at them sometimes and I find it funny because you can't swear at a spirit; they just brush it off and ignore her. I guess they just allow her to vent sometimes.

Some of my mom's friends have spirits and I assume they all must have some, but I only see a few of them. One of her friends even meditates with his spirits. I'm not sure what that means, but it brings him great comfort and enables him to help lots of other people.

One of my dog acquaintances poo-poos the idea of spirits. He thinks we are all crazy and not able to take care of ourselves so we make up a spirit world.

He is always out of control, never gets off leash and is caged in his kennel almost all the time because his humans can't trust him anywhere in the house. If he'd only look to his spirit and acknowledge his spirit, he could have a wonderful life.

Rita - Spirits

I HAVE NO IDEA WHY we are brought into this world. Aren't there enough cats, dogs and humans here already?

I also have no idea why we need to have spirits to guide us. Seems to me, we all should be able to make it on our own. This world is not that difficult to handle.

But, what really bothers me is why in the hell do our spirits think we need to have some purpose and sign a contract promising to fulfill that contract? Aren't we good enough to decide for ourselves what we want?

Anyway, what is a contract? If it's akin to ones humans make, it can be broken anytime. I always thought that's why contracts were made—to be broken.

I was still very young when my spirit contacted me. She said my contract was to get my championship papers, give my breeders two litters of pups and then compete on the dog show circuit and bring home a best in show for my breeders.

For crying out loud, my eyes were barely open and this spirit comes and wants to plan my whole life for me; don't I get a say in matters of this importance?

Since I didn't know what all that meant or entailed anyway, I said, yeah, sure, okay, whatever. Sure didn't seem like a big deal to me. Who was this spirit thing hanging around me and would it ever go away?

The answer is no; that spirit never leaves you. Lots of dogs never even know they have a spirit; why did I have to be one of the unlucky ones who not only sees my spirit, but has to listen to her too?

You know, I did most of the things on that list and I did them well. However, I really didn't want to do the dog show bit. I didn't want to disappoint my breeders, but they had other dogs who liked doing that sort of thing.

I asked my spirit if it would be possible to enter into a new contract with them that wouldn't involve dog shows. They said no, once a contract is broken, you cannot enter into a new one with them and must suffer the consequences.

Suffer the consequences? What did that mean? The spirit told me that there might be a chance of a new contract with someone else and I said that sounded fine. I figured if I could get out of one contract, I could get out of another if I wanted.

My spirit warned me that you don't get many chances to make a contract for your purpose in the world and if you kept breaking those contracts, you wouldn't be around too long.

So, what? If I didn't keep my contract, I would die? I would die sometime anyway. What a bunch of malarkey.

My spirit told me about a woman who had lost her dog—a whippet named Andrew. Andrew's spirit was looking for someone to replace him. I chuckled; it would not be hard to follow in a male's paw prints, so I asked for more information.

Andrew's contract with her was to protect her and teach her about unconditional love. It was pretty easy stuff and I figured he'd trained her pretty well, so I wouldn't have much to do.

Part of my contract was that I would have to be her companion, and since she already knew about unconditional love, I was to help her regain her purpose and passion in life. I had no idea what that meant, so I asked my spirit if she would help me do that. She said yes, but I would have to stick by her and not go out on my own.

Okay, okay, can't be that difficult to handle. Besides, I needed to get out of the dog shows.

I didn't know if I should ask, but, it was my life we were talking about and I needed to know what would be in it for me.

My spirit explained that this woman was retired and had a lot of time to take me for walks and maybe even let me chase rabbits and squirrels. That didn't seem like such a big deal because I never got to chase squirrels and rabbits anyway. What else was in it for me?

I was told I would be able to go fishing, hiking and camping with her and see places I never dreamed of. I didn't know how to fish, camp or hike, so why would I be interested in those things?

And, see places I never dreamed of—how silly. If you've never dreamed of something, why would you want to see it? So far I wasn't hearing anything about what I might want to do. It was as though everyone else was planning what they thought I would like. Of course, I had no idea of what I wanted.

My spirit said I would be the center of her life because she didn't have many family members left and the ones she had lived far away. There was no significant other in her life. I interrupted and asked what a significant other was. She said it would be like I felt having Timmy in my life. I guess that meant she would not be having any pups.

Speaking of pups, would I have to have any more litters. My spirit said no—I had already done that.

So, that was it? That was all there was in it for me. I was just supposed to be there for a woman who seemed to have nothing.

My spirit reminded me the main reason for the contract was so I could bring purpose and passion back into her life.

How would I bring something into her life that she should have obtained on her own?

My spirit pointed out that everything I did, I did with a great amount of passion; I didn't do anything half-way. My human would be able to see this and understand she needed more passion in her life. As for the purpose, my spirit said she would work with the human's spirit, but once she had passion back in her life, the purpose would follow. Maybe the human's purpose was to write books and help others.

Plus, the spirit said, she has flannel sheets on the bed.

That sealed it—I agreed and signed a new contract.

She came to see me and I liked her and the jerky treats. But, I was a little upset when she dumped me in her truck and drove me away from my home. I guess I thought she would move in with me and do all those things.

I can see my human's spirits—she has several of them. She claims she can't see them. One of them is this skinny woman with long hair. She reminds me of someone, but I don't know who. She doesn't say much to me. I think she's trying to be the quiet, dignified side of my human.

There's one short, ugly dude who thinks he's funny, but I think he's an idiot. He's always playing tricks on my human and laughing a lot. He kind of reminds me of Martin Short. You didn't know I knew Martin?

David has tons of spirits. He brought them over to the house one time, along with this big bowl. He sat on the floor and spun something around inside it and it made a lot of noise. He says the noise bothers Koki and Osito, but I was rather intrigued by it. He also blessed our house while he was here. I guess that's to keep evil spirits away from me.

I followed him around the house and he kept seeing different colored lights in each room. He only found one corner that didn't have good colored lights. I think that was the corner I saw Charlie spray one time.

I'm not scared by the lights, of course, I don't see colors, just lights and I'm not scared by the sound the bowl makes. There isn't much that scares me.

I'm still not all that sure about my spirit. She has helped me with the passion thing. I'm so passionate about many things, like chasing squirrels and rabbits. I don't do anything stoically. I run wild turkeys off away from my house. I steal food from my dog friends when I visit at their houses. Sometimes, I try to sneak out with one of their toys. I have a large number of humans trained to give me treats when I bless them with my presence.

When humans give me treats, I expect to get three of them, and I can count. I get a little annoyed with one or two, unless they are big, chewy delicious treats.

I eat ice cubes as though they were the best tasting things in the world. I've been known to steal things like toys from cats and dogs that I know. I eat chickens like they were only brought into this world for me to enjoy. Fridays at Safeway are five dollar chicken days. I always go with my human and make sure she picks up at least five of those suckers.

My human bones them out, puts them in baggies and freezes them for me. I never run out of chicken. Just once, I'd give anything for her to bone out a chicken and place all the meat in my bowl so I can see how fast I can consume it all. Probably would make me sick, but I've eaten other things that made me sick and decided in the end, it was worth it.

I sleep soundly and peacefully, like I don't have a care in the world. I think my passion is rubbing off on my human. If only she weren't as passionate about being in charge as I am.

That's a problem when you have two bitches that are passionate about the same things, but I think we both have found the struggle for dominance to be a lot of fun.

As for her purpose, she thinks she can write, so she is writing books. When she told me she was going to finish the book Andrew had started, I jumped right in and explained that I should be the one to finish it. Why would we want any stupid human ideas in our book?

I did check with my spirit and she said writing a book might be good therapy for me and help me understand my place. Is my spirit crazy, or what?

Andrew - Unconditional Love

WHAT A WONDERFUL THING UNCONDITIONAL love is, and only animals can give it. Perhaps that is why we are so adored by humans. It is easy to do and comes naturally. Even humans who aren't nice are loved unconditionally by their animal friends.

Not all animals can love unconditionally—cats come to mind. I don't know what is wrong with cats, but they are too self-centered to love without conditions. I'm sure they are on this earth for a reason, but I can't think of one.

Don't get me wrong, I loved Susan, but I'm not certain she was a real cat. I think she was sent here from some alien planet to see how humans lived. If she sent back any messages to her people, they would have thought she had gone mad, so they just stranded her here.

There were times you could walk past Susan, look her in the eye, or wag your tail in front of her face, and there would be no reaction. She wasn't home, as they say. I don't know where she went during those times, but she was out there somewhere.

I loved her unconditionally, too, but was glad I didn't have to depend on her for anything.

When she started being sick, I wanted to cry. I knew she was probably going back to her planet soon. Our vet came to the house to help send Susan on her trip back home. It made me wonder if the vet was an alien too.

I had to be locked in the laundry room while the vet was here because I didn't want her near Susan. The night before that, I had let Susan go into my kennel. I always knew she wanted in there, so I let her do it. Our human took a picture and started crying. The next day, Susan was gone. I'm so glad she got to see my kennel from the inside.

My human told me Susan was gone, but I kept looking for her. Then, we went outside and I was shown a place where my human said she buried Susan. I don't know what that was all about. I assumed she took a space craft back to her planet.

Every so often, I go outside and wander over to where Susan was buried. I miss her; she was so weird.

I love my mom. I've been calling her that for some time now. She has become so much more than just my human. It is easy to give her unconditional love, and she needs it.

I never criticize her for anything or complain when she goes golfing all the time. Actually, when she's gone, I get to have some time for myself and rest without worrying about what she's up to—nice break.

If she eats or drinks too much, do I condemn or ridicule her? No, but I do laugh at her if she's feeling under the weather because she ate too much of things she knows she shouldn't eat. Of course, I understand that. Given the chance, I would always eat more of something I liked and worry about getting sick later.

I love to ride in the car with her, even when we're not going any place fun. Errands can be a drag, but I know she appreciates me being there with her. It is interesting to listen to her talk when she drives. I know she's not always talking to me, but I'm not sure who she is talking to. It sounds as though she's talking to people in other cars, but that's kind of silly because they can't hear her.

Oh, well, if it makes her feel good, I listen. Usually, after accompanying her while she does human things, we get to stop and do important dog things, like run through fields and chase rabbits and squirrels.

There's this one place she takes me and when she talks about it to other humans, they spell the name of the place—W-I-L-S-O-N P-A-R-K. I laugh and pretend like I don't know what she's talking about, but all us dogs know. Granted, I may not know exactly how to spell, but when humans spell, you know you are in for a treat. You know, like I-C-E C-R-E-A-M.

That first letter, W, has a unique sound. No mistaking where we are going. She doesn't even have to spell the rest of the word. We dogs love going there because of all the rabbits.

The place is huge and wide open. There are fences all around it, but they are far away and the only time you get near one is if you happen to chase a rabbit all the way there. They can escape because they can fit through the fence and we can't. There is one little dog who goes out there and she could fit through the fence, but she can't run that far.

There is an unofficial scoreboard out there. Unofficial because it is not supposed to be there and especially because of what it's for. Humans in this area say they abhor the idea of dogs chasing and killing rabbits, but they won't do anything about the booming population, and those suckers sure know how to have babies.

Apparently, it is against the law to shoot or poison rabbits, so letting the dogs have a good time is the best solution, and we love it. The hawks love it too because if we catch one, they come down and take it home for dinner.

If you get a rabbit, your human slinks behind this big bush and marks down a score next to your name. In December, we have a big party and the winner for the year receives this huge milk bone—and I mean huge; you can hardly carry it.

I won it four years in a row. I lost the first three years to Lucy, a greyhound. She had longer legs than I did and the girl was fast. Then, she got old and I kept beating her out.

Every time I got that huge milk bone, I wanted to take it home, but all the other dogs wanted a part of it. I'd try to run with that big thing in my mouth, but I'd have to keep running around the car until my mom got there. She was so slow.

It's too bad that humans can't give unconditional love, but for some reason, they can't. I know my mom learned a lot from me, but she never learned how to love unconditionally. She came close to loving me unconditionally, but at times, she did have conditions. I couldn't always do everything I wanted to, but I sure let her do what she wanted.

She was always able to show me that she loved me, even up to the end when she had to make the decision to let me go because I was suffering. I think in that final moment she realized she could love unconditionally.

I've seen and met a lot of humans in my life and I still can't figure out how they love each other. They all have a different definition of love and they all show it in different ways. It has to be one of the most confusing emotions they have.

Humans say they love each other and then turn around and hit each other, and I don't mean a love pat. They love each other so much they will kill so that person can't love anyone else.

They have children out of love they say, and then they abuse their child. Are they crazy?

Maybe someday humans will truly learn how to love unconditionally, but I doubt it. They would have to rid themselves of too many conditions.

Meanwhile, I'm so glad I'm a dog and can love without restrictions. For me, true love comes when I can crawl into those flannel sheets and snuggle up with my mom.

Rita - Unconditional Love

YEAH, YEAH, YEAH—UNCONDITIONAL LOVE; IT'S really not all it's made out to be. Unconditional love only works if you get what you want. It would be a really big thing if humans could do it, but they can't, so why should we expend all that time and energy on something that can't be reciprocated?

The only reason dogs think it's cool is because it is a sure fire way to get what we want. Not all animals can do it, though. Cats, for example, can no more give unconditional love than a cistern can. Okay, so I don't know what a cistern is, but I do know, you sure don't see them in anyone's home.

I wish I had known Andrew's cat, not that she loved unconditionally, but because she was a space cadet—my kind of people. She didn't really make too many demands on anyone. She didn't do too much of anything.

No, I'm stuck with stupid old Charlie. I don't think he loves anything, except food. That creature whines, complains, swats at you, sprays in your direction and does all sorts of distasteful things if he doesn't get his way.

He has no intention of loving anyone, conditionally or not, well, except maybe me. I'm sooooo hard to resist and I let him think I'm on his side in all the arguments with my human. In reality, I could care less about him and he could less about everything.

I can love unconditionally. It's what I'm supposed to do naturally. And, I'm good at letting humans think I love them unconditionally, but I've learned a few things from Charlie, and I too, have some conditions.

As long as I'm in charge and have things going my way, I will love you with all my heart and soul.

Keep flannel sheets on the bed and I'll let you sleep with me.

Feed me more of the chicken you fix (you can have the wings) and I'll clean your hands every night.

Take me out hunting every day and I will impress you with my speed.

Don't let it rain every day so I'm stuck in the house all day and maybe I'll listen to more of your idiotic stories about humans I don't even know.

Always let me ride shotgun even when a friend of yours is with us and I won't try and sit on your lap.

Let me sneak out to the sun room once in a while to steal Charlie's food and I'll tell him not to spray any of your things.

You see, in order to love unconditionally, there just has to be some conditions along the way. If humans could love without conditions, imagine what the world would be like. Opps, maybe I'll take that back. If humans could love unconditionally, why would they need dogs?

One of the most appealing things about having a dog is that humans believe we give them unconditional love, and we let them think that. How hard is it to act all excited and pleased when our humans come home?

Humans can't do the same things to each other because sometimes they aren't happy when someone comes home. Even if a dog isn't happy, they will pretend to be. It takes such little effort to get up off the bed, run quickly, wagging ones tail and greet a human. I mean, really, ten seconds out of your day and the humans get such a big bang out of it.

The one time humans come close to being able to give unconditional love is when they are visited by dogs in hospitals and convalescent homes. Some of my friends do that. Maybe I'll try it someday.

These old people who are nearing the end of their life can reach out to a dog in ways they never could to another human and a special bond is formed. Everyone wins in these situations. Both the dog and the human, at least for a brief moment in time, are able to share that feeling of unconditional love.

When I moved in with my human, I let it be known that I would be the head bitch in control. Oh, she tries real hard to be the head honcho, and I let her think she is, but that's just part of my plan to get my way.

I don't mind if she goes golfing, out to dinner with her friends (most of whom have dogs in their homes who are controlling matters), but, when she comes back, it is so easy to make her feel guilty about leaving me. It's to the point that she feels so guilty, I get to chose where I want to go rabbit hunting.

My human thinks if she lets me chase rabbits, I'll wear myself out and I'll behave better. BEHAVE? Are you serious? I'll get to go out again, after I rest a bit. I will admit, though, that chasing rabbits does tire me out and I am a lot calmer the rest of the day. Not too much bothers me if I've been able to do some chasing.

If she ever tells me no, or tries to get me to do something I don't want to do, I wiggle my nose at her, kind of like that lady did on bewitched. It doesn't always work, but sometimes she laughs and forgets what she wanted me to do.

Sometimes, my human makes me so mad I could spit. What really bums me out most is that sometimes, she doesn't get it. She has no idea why I'm so angry. If she'd stop and think for one moment, she'd know why I was mad. Other times, she does know why I'm mad, but she won't do anything about it.

Who is in charge here?

I'll sit on the floor next to her bed and stare at her—she can't stand that. My eyes never blink; I just stare, so she turns away from me. Now that pisses me off.

So, I go and get one of my beds (I have two), and place one on top of the other. I do that because to sit on just one bed does not make it high enough for her to see me if she's on her bed. With one on top of the other, she can't help but see me sitting there, staring at her.

When she still won't budge, I go around the house and collect all my friends, my stuffed animals and toys. I place them all on the bed, with all of them looking in her direction.

One time, Charlie was using one of my beds for a nap and I made him move. He got the idea of what I was up to and climbed up on the bed with all my other friends. Of course, being a stupid cat, he lay down and went back to sleep instead of starting at our human.

And, there we all sit, me and all my friends, and there she sits—with no one! If she weren't so mean, she could have friends on the bed with her.

Finally, she'll get up, go to the kitchen and take some ice cream out of the freezer. I'm right there behind her to remind her to get two spoons. I dump my friends, jump on the bed and eat ice cream with her. Afterwards, I get to lick the bowl.

And that, my friends is how unconditional love works.

Andrew - Vet Visits

ONE OF THE UNFORTUNATE THINGS about being a dog is that sometimes you have to go see the vet.

We used to have this cartoon on the wall by my food dish. It shows Marmaduke hanging out the window of a car his human is driving. He sees a friend on the street and calls, "I'll be right back as soon as I get tutored."

I never knew what was funny about that, and I certainly saw no humor in it after I went to get "tutored." One minute you are awake wondering what's going on, and the next thing you know, you wake up wondering what happened to your missing parts.

Getting tutored means you lose the family jewels, not that I know what that means. Was there something wrong with them? I was groggy for three days and didn't feel like doing anything. I kept looking to see what was missing, but I couldn't tell.

After I recovered from that ordeal, I realized I no longer had the urge to hump bushes. I guess that's a good thing because I never knew why I did it.

One positive thing about getting tutored is you don't have to get tutored twice.

I liked my vet. She was soft-spoken and kind and treated me like I was the only dog in the world. She was Susan's vet, too, and one time, she called my mom and told her a couple had come in named Susan and Andrew and they had a dog named Lucky. My mom's name was Luckii. Those people didn't know how to name a dog, obviously.

Fortunately, trips to the vet don't happen too often. They are usually six or seven years apart (in dog years). I always cried when they gave me a shot. It makes humans feel sorry for what they did to you. The vet always tries to give you a treat after they shoot you, examine you, or stick that thing up your rear end.

Susan had told me not to take any treats from the vet because they want you to like them and come back for more pain and suffering. I didn't know if Susan was just pulling my leg or not. It was hard to turn down a treat, but Susan warned me.

Vet visits are never any fun, no matter how much you like your vet. First of all, there is no warning. You are out for a nice ride in the car and the next thing you know; you are being dragged into the vet office. Maybe it's best not to know in advance; saves time you have to worry about what they'll do to you.

Once you're in there, there's no place for a dog to sit. Oh, they have chairs and benches, but the humans sit there. We are supposed to sit on the floor, I guess. The floors are always cold and hard; sometimes they are a little wet because someone had an accident.

You have to sit patiently and listen to other dogs complain and hear the cats yowling even before anyone does anything to them. All that does is make you more nervous.

In the examination room, once again, there's no comfortable place to sit. I used to climb up on the bench and hide behind mom, but they always found me.

When they placed you on the table, it was hard and cold. You'd think maybe they could have put a flannel sheet on it to make it more bearable.

My mom and I often went fishing. I didn't know how to do it at first and I was leery about getting in the boat. Susan had said the boat was only good for hiding in and staying out of the rain and not to get in it if it wasn't on land.

But, if I wanted to go along, I had to get in the boat. I learned to like it a lot. I had my bed and food dish with me and mom always had water for me to drink. I thought the water thing was overkill because I didn't need a bowl of water when I had a whole lake to drink from.

I didn't help much with the fishing, except when mom landed a fish; I'd lick it before she put it in the ice chest. Later, we'd cook them and eat them.

I always had to go to the vet after we went fishing or camping. I had to take pills for something called giardia. Mom said I got it from drinking water out of the lake. It made me have terrible diarrhea. But, lake water always tasted so good.

One day when mom was at work, I went out to the sun room to explore. I saw all our fishing gear stuck in one corner of the room and decided to investigate.

This little box with all her toys and trinkets was partially open, so I looked in. There were all kinds of pretty gizmos with colored beads and long things that flashed when the light hit them. They were the things mom would put on the end of her fishing pole.

One of the beaded items caught my attention. I pulled it out for a closer look. What a big mistake.

On the end of the beads was the hook—the one she used to nail fish with. It got caught in my nose. Damn, that hurt. I didn't know what to do. I was pretty sure I was going to be in trouble for snooping where I shouldn't have been, but what was I going to do with this hook in my nose?

I went back in the house and decided to sit in the laundry room; surely I was going to doggie prison for this act.

Susan came in and laughed at me. It wasn't funny. She came over, smelled the hook, made a face and opened her mouth, but, as usual, no sound came out.

Finally, I went and tried to lie down on my bed, but I couldn't put my head down, so I wasn't comfortable. I ended up just sitting there and waiting.

When mom came home, she took one look at me, gasped and then laughed. It wasn't funny. Why did everyone think a hook in your nose was funny?

The vet put me to sleep and when I woke up, the hook was mysteriously gone. What a relief. Guess I'll leave all the fishing gear for her. Wonder if she ever had a hook stuck in her nose?

The worst experience I ever had with the vet occurred one morning when I was walking with mom. We were near one of the fields where I chased rabbits. The sun was starting to come up, which is a good time for rabbit hunting. Before I was let off the leash, I decided I better dump so I could run faster. I didn't like humans to watch, so I moved to the edge of the road and mom walked as far away as the leash would take her.

All of a sudden, I felt something hit me and everything went black. The next thing I knew, I was in mom's arms. She was crying and swearing. She thought I was dead. Apparently some guy named asshole (that's what she called him), came around the corner too fast, swerved and hit me with his truck. He didn't stop or anything.

Since I didn't want mom to think I was dead, I whimpered. She ran home, put me in the car and we drove to a hospital at the university. I later learned it was the veterinary school's teaching hospital and one of the best in the country. Mom said it was one of two places in the country that could have saved my life. Wonder where the other one is?

They put me in intensive care, told my mom I probably wouldn't make it through the night and to call the next day. I knew I wasn't going home.

Some woman that mom golfed with was a very important person at this hospital and she came to oversee how they were treating me. They ran tests and did all sorts of things. I think they gave me something for pain because I didn't feel anything. I didn't feel good.

Obviously, I didn't die. I had to live, my mom needed me and I had not finished fulfilling my contract with her. They wouldn't let her see me because they thought it would be too upsetting for both of us.

After about a week, they let me go home, but I couldn't do much. Mom had to carry me outside to do my business and I made her carry me all the way to the neighbor's yard. She said I could do it on my own lawn, but I didn't like that idea. I spent too much time lying out there in the sun; I didn't want it messed up in any way.

I wasn't home too long before I had to go back to the hospital for some surgery. They had to put a steel plate somewhere in my hip. I guess my timing was perfect because the hospital had one of the best orthopedic surgeons visiting there for a while. He was able to use my surgery to show other vets how it's done.

By the time I saw my mom again, I was starting to feel better, wasn't in a constant fog and could actually walk. I was so excited to see her that as I walked, I peed on the floor. Guess that did the trick—I never had to go back there again. If I'd known that was all it would take, I would have peed on the floor the first day.

Although it seemed like it took forever to fully recover, I suppose in human terms it was a few weeks. Mom was always there taking care of me.

She even took me to work with her sometimes so I wouldn't get lonely. She was painting houses and it was really boring watching paint dry.

I had to take a bunch of pills. I guess it was so I wouldn't get an infection or something. She would hide them in chicken. I knew they were there, but, I loved chicken, so I did as I was told. Eventually, she gave me the chicken without the pills.

Apparently, they did a good job on me because I was able to chase rabbits again and I wasn't in any pain.

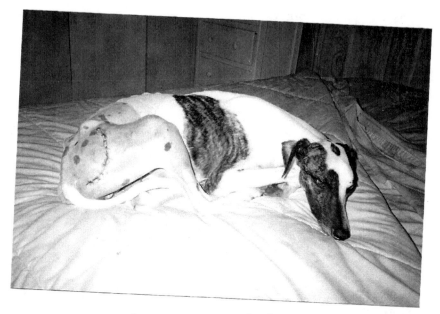

Andrew recuperating after his surgery

Rita - Vet Visits

After my hysterectomy, I figured that would be it for vet visits. What else could they do to me? I was told I couldn't have any more pups, so why would I need to go back? What a relief—no more pups. I guess that also meant no more fun with Timmy, but I hadn't seen him in a long time, so it was no big loss.

Of course, I did find out I had to go back every so often for shots and heartworm medicine, but, I didn't like going to the vet. I hated that place. I shook and trembled every time we came near the door, and I was always looking for a way out. Someone would open the door and I'd make a mad dash for it.

Some dogs like to socialize while they are in the waiting room. What idiots! Didn't they understand why they were there? It is not a fun place to be, like the doggie park, and I didn't want to play with them or anyone. I tried to pretend I wasn't there and wished they would pretend I wasn't there also.

The yappers are the most annoying; they never shut up. I don't know if they are just nervous or are being friendly. Either way, it pissed me off and I'd bark at them, but that didn't stop them.

When I had to go to the vet, I wanted in right now. No need to stop and weigh me. Do whatever had to be done and let me get the hell out. My human totally understood.

When we were through, I'd go outside and piss on the bush near the door. From the smell of it, I wasn't the only one doing that.

My human would always take me to the overcrossing and let me take out my anger on the squirrels.

49

I wonder if my human gets as nervous when she has to go to her vet?

Sometimes when I'm chasing rabbits, I get so focused, so excited and so enthralled with what I'm doing, I don't always look where I'm going; it doesn't enter my mind.

We had been out to a field one day, loaded with rabbits and I was having the time of my life. It was hard to decide which way to run because they were going in so many different directions. At one point, I thought I ran into something, but I wasn't sure and I wasn't going to stop and check. Whatever it was, it didn't hurt, so I kept going.

After we arrived home, I decided to go out and lie in the sun and rest. It is one of my favorite things to do. I love to lie there and look dead. People go by and talk to me and I never even flinch. Someone is always telling my human they think something is wrong with me. I chuckle.

A neighbor stopped by to see my human, so I didn't get up. They were sitting outside talking. I rolled over on my back and started scratching. It felt so good.

The neighbor got all upset and started yelling. Now, how's a girl supposed to get a nap with all that noise? She screamed that a piece of pipe was hanging out of my underarm and there was blood.

Oh, maybe that was the thing I ran into earlier. It was staring to hurt a little and I could see the blood.

Of course, that meant another trip to the vet and my human went into action. Here's a big tip about vet visits. If your human takes you there and leaves you there, you are in big trouble. If she stays with you the whole time, you'll be out of there soon.

My human stayed while they removed the pipe and stitched me up. I figured that was it and I was good as new. But, stitches mean restrictions. There must be some other way to fix things besides stitches.

So, now I wouldn't be able to run and chase rabbits and I'd have to take those terrible pills again for another eternity, even after I know I'm all well.

Humans are prone to overkill. Not that I understand why a dog ever needs to take pills, but when we do, it's usually to ward off some kind of infection or something. Humans insist you take the pills faithfully for ten days.

Any dog in its right mind knows the pills are not needed for that long. When I knew I had taken enough pills, I balked at taking more, but my human insisted I finish them. No amount of peanut butter makes it fun for that long.

Have you ever had an Elizabethan collar? Where did they ever come up with that name for such an ugly contraption? Some sadist named Elizabeth probably thought of it. They should have called it a deadly head vice. You can be sure a dog never invented it.

I had been given one after my hysterectomy, so my human said we didn't need another one. I knew she wouldn't put it on me. The first time, I purposely knocked things over and ran into my human until her leg finally bled, and sat on my bed for hours staring at her.

Even ice cream wouldn't help because how in the hell can you eat ice cream with that damn thing on? And, who would want to eat ice cream then anyway?

One thing did come to mind, however. Why not fill the collar up with ice cream and let it run down into your mouth as it melted. Now, that might be a good use for the collar.

I promised my human not to bother any stitches or injured areas if I didn't have to wear the collar. She believed me and never, ever saw me go near the wound.

By now, everyone must know I am an intelligent girl, so, it's not unreasonable to assume that I had learned my lesson, and I had. But, different situations arise in a busy girl's life that are unexpected. I did learn not to run into pipes, but other things do happen.

One of the places we often go in the afternoons is the golf annex. Humans like to give names to places that have no names. They do this so they can communicate with each other exactly where they are heading. Like dogs don't also learn the names so we know where they are taking us?

The golf annex is near a golf course (how original). You can actually see a couple of holes from where we run, but there are fences to keep us out of the course. It's more like the fences are to keep the humans from sneaking in and playing for free.

There's a road alongside the fence and next to the road are several large, empty fields. Well, they aren't always empty; sometimes there are crops growing in them.

It's fun to sneak into the fenced area because all the squirrels live there and occasionally, a rabbit will hide in the bushes. Plus that, it is a lot harder for the humans to get through the fence to get us.

Koki and I were in the fenced area chasing squirrels. Osito was with the humans, begging treats and looking for fresh rabbit droppings. It was like caviar to her.

We scared a rabbit out of a bush and it started running for the fence. I was excited because as soon as it got through, it would head for the open fields and I'd have a better chance of catching it.

Squirrels either run up a tree or jump into their holes to avoid me, but rabbits run forever.

As I came to the bush the rabbit had gone through, I saw it was one of those big prickly, thistle bushes that hurt a lot if you run into them, so I jumped over the bush.

I thought I was clear until I landed on the barbed wire fence next to the bush. Damn, one of the barbs stuck in my chest and I couldn't get loose.

The humans came running. They seemed upset. They were both trying to get the barb out of me and it was taking too long; the rabbit was getting away. They finally unhooked me and set me on the ground.

My human reached for the water she had brought and as she took the cap off, I took off after the rabbit. I knew I would never catch up to it, but I kept running because I was pretty sure when I got back, we'd have to go home.

I was right, we had to go home. My human took a towel she had and tried to clean me up. There wasn't that much blood, but she wanted to see how deep my wounds were. She was only concerned about the one in my chest where the barb nailed me.

Fortunately, it was too late to go to the vet. My human cleaned me more after we got home and put some Neosporin on my cuts. That stuff always made me feel better. I think we must have a dozen tubes of it around the house. One of us is always dinging themself, it seems.

My human did some energy work on me that night. She's good at it and it is so relaxing. I usually fall asleep while she's working on me. I don't know how many times I've hurt myself and her energy work keeps me from having to go to the vet. She can do it on herself too. Later, I'll tell you how she healed herself after a horrible fall, but right now, this is about me.

The next morning, she decided the hole in my chest was too big to ignore. She was afraid it might get infected. I knew it would heal just fine, but off to the vet we went. It was time for more stitches, pills and limited running and hunting.

The vet keeps telling me what a tough cookie I am and wonders why I seem to come in every April for a visit.

I'll tell you why things happen to dogs in April. It has been raining all winter and then the sun comes out. Everything starts to grow quickly and uncontrollably. The weeds can get six feet high in less than a week. Thistles spread out everywhere and hurt your feet when you walk on them.

It isn't easy to chase rabbits through all the vegetation. I have to leap in the air to get above the growing things and when I come down, I have no idea where I'll land.

If those lazy humans would get off their butts and get out and mow all the crap down, I wouldn't be at the vet office every April.

Andrew - Grief

GRIEF IS SOMETHING EVERYONE CAN understand, even animals. It is not just a human emotion. When a dog loses its human it is one of the most devastating things in their life. I have heard of dogs that stop eating, drinking water and chasing rabbits because their human is gone.

One of my mom's friends died and his dog died two weeks later of a broken heart. Most dogs, however, learn to cope and go on with their lives.

I had a friend named Myrtle. She was staying with some people she liked and her mom died while on a trip somewhere. Myrtle never understood why her mom didn't come back, but she made a new life for herself.

After I got hit by that truck, my mom told our neighbor, Nellie, she didn't know what she would have done if I had died.

Nellie looked at her and said, "Why, you selfish bitch. You better hope he goes before you. He would be lost without you and never understand why you deserted him. You understand death and would survive, not that anyone would want to be around you after that, but you would recover."

That old lady was right, you know. I would have thought she left me because she didn't love me anymore.

When Nellie got sick, she had to move to a convalescent hospital. We used to go visit her. She always remembered me and would scratch me when I visited.

I didn't like the place where she was staying. There were a lot of old, lost people there.

Nellie started to forget lots of things, but there were two things she remembered until her dying day. She always remembered my name and that at some point in the day, she would get her toddy. Her doctor wrote a prescription so she could have her Canadian mist every afternoon. Though she no longer remembered what time she was to get it, they always gave it to her.

One day we were visiting and she said, "Andrew, how good to see you." She looked at mom and said, "What are you doing with my neighbor's dog?"

It was so sad, but mom replied, "She couldn't make it so I brought Andrew over to see you."

After Nellie died, mom took me to the cemetery and showed me her grave. She said Nellie was in a better place and we were so fortunate to have known her. I sure missed her scratching me because she had long fingernails and it felt so good.

Losing Susan was hard, not because we had become good friends, but because she was special. She wasn't your typical cat and I still think she was from outer space.

Time was when the dogs in our town were allowed to run free in the back part of the cemetery. I had such fond memories of that place and so many of the wonderful dogs I met. Most of them moved on to some other place, and a few of them died.

Spotty was a good friend of mine. We were the same age. In the winter, huge pools of water would form at the cemetery and I loved to get Spotty chasing me. I'd jump over the water, but he'd run right through it and come out all wet and muddy. His mom used to blame me for it.

One day, after I'd recovered from being hit by that truck, Spotty was hit by a car. He didn't fare so well and died. It was hard to imagine life without him.

In December, his mom held a funeral service for him out at Wilson Park. He spent a lot of time there, chasing rabbits. A lot of people showed up and brought their dogs.

We weren't sure why we were there, but it seemed like a good time to run and chase rabbits. The humans gathered under some kind of canopy and told stories about Spotty. We didn't pay too much attention until they brought out the treats.

Of course, we wanted the same things the humans were eating, but they had special ones for us.

Spotty had been cremated and his ashes were spread out over the park. I always knew he was there when I'd go back out.

Mom told me that when I died, she was going to have me cremated and when she died, she was going to be cremated. Both of us would have our ashes scattered over our favorite fishing hole and we'd be together forever.

I didn't understand all of that cremation stuff, but I relished the thought that even after we died, we'd be together.

Most of the time I never had to experience the death of a human. Mom would tell me about one of the dogs from the park who died, but I usually knew they were old and ready to go.

Eddie was a different story, however. He had been a dog who was dumped out in the fields outside of town, and two of my mom's friends had rescued him. We had become friends because of our moms. It was fun when his moms went away and we got to dog sit. We would take him to Wilson Park because he never got to go there. We'd let him off the leash and let him run. He loved that.

I tried to teach him how to hunt rabbits, but he wasn't that interested. He just liked to run and didn't care which direction he went. Just as well, I guess; it left all the rabbits for me.

He became very ill and had to have an operation, so we went to visit him. I took one look at him and couldn't believe my eyes. One of his legs was missing—the whole leg, all the way to his shoulder. How was he supposed to run?

However, he did real well, and it was only a few days after his surgery. He could jump up on the couch and could run pretty fast with only three legs. I wondered if I'd be able to do as well with only three legs. It sure would give the rabbits a fighting chance.

That was the last time I saw Eddie. He died shortly thereafter and I had lost another friend.

Mom was losing lots of her friends. She would always tell me about someone she knew who had died. Sometimes she would cry and sometimes, she'd swear.

She had gone golfing one day with her dad and when she came home, he wasn't with her. She paced through the house, crying, swearing and yelling. Her dad had died on the sixteenth tee at the course they were playing.

Mom was beside herself with grief. There was nothing I could do to console her, so I made her take me rabbit hunting. She cried the whole time we were at Wilson Park. When we came home, she fixed herself a drink and became very quiet.

I hadn't known her parents too well, but after her dad died, her mom would come and visit often. She liked me a lot and always brought or sent gifts, treats, cards and letters to me. She said I was her favorite grandson.

We would drive up to Oregon to visit her mom. She had to move out of her house into a foster care home with some other old people. The last time we saw her, she wasn't doing too well. I knew she wouldn't be around much longer, so I gave her a kiss when we left.

I knew I would miss grandma, but I wondered how mom was going to take it.

By the time, grandma died, I was on my downhill path. I had a bad heart and was getting old too. I couldn't do things I used to do. Mom had to go to Oregon for her mom's memorial service. I couldn't go because it was too long of a trip for me. One of her friends came and took care of me. I hoped mom would be okay and hurry back to me. She did.

Less than a month later, mom had to put me to sleep. We both knew it was time. I didn't want to leave her, but I had to. Somehow, I knew she would be strong, but the timing really sucked.

Humans don't always deal with their grief as well as they should. Some of them literally go crazy, lose their sense of direction and blame everyone and everything for their loss.

My mom was strong; she would survive. I know she went away to a golf tournament after I died, and I was glad she did, but when she came home; our whole carport was filled with flowers, pictures of me, cards and even some stuffed animals.

I loved the stuffed animal tribute. Everyone knew I had a lot of stuffed animal friends—all with the squeaky thing still in them. I used to carry them with me when we went for walks. The only hard thing was deciding which one to take.

No one knew I had taken one with me when I died. It was my green dinosaur. I called him Dino. All my friends had names. When I would carry Niles, my stuffed squirrel, people would look shocked because they thought he was real.

I wasn't able to tell mom that Dino had gone with me, but she knew he was gone. She looked all over the house for him when she was putting my toys away. She was really upset and had a friend come over to help her look for him.

Her friend jokingly mentioned that maybe Dino had gone with me, but she knew that hadn't happened and was terribly beside herself over not finding him.

Maybe when she reads this she'll understand why she never found Dino. And, by the way, Dino was not cremated.

One day I had been carrying Dino and some woman almost ran her car off the road when she saw us. She was laughing real hard and waved. Later that day, mom was at a store and this woman stopped and asked if she had a dog that carried a green dinosaur around. She admitted that she did. The woman replied, "I saw him today, almost ran off the road I was laughing so hard. I'd had a miserable morning and that just made my day. Thank him for me."

Rita - Grief

WELL, GOOD GRIEF! WHAT IS all this nonsense about grief? Humans are so sensitive about death. Surely they know that life is not complete without death. What would this world be like if there were no death?

When someone dies, humans make memorials for them, usually at the place where they died. They leave flowers, cards, toys, even food. How in the heck do they expect the dead to come and get all those things?

Personally, the hard thing for dogs to do when their human dies is to have enough time left themselves to train someone new. This is especially true if you have done a great job of training your human. Some of us are masters at it and I would hate to lose my human because she knows my every want and need. I can get her to do just about anything I want, and I never have to give as much back. I hope she doesn't read this part.

I almost lost my human a while ago; at least I thought I did. We had been together long enough for me to have her trained. We were at a golf tournament and she fell down a flight of concrete stairs, head first.

I was waiting in the car for her to come and take me for a ride in the golf cart, so I didn't see the incident, but I heard the ambulance and wondered what had happened.

When one of her friends came to get me and not her, I knew something was wrong. We went over to the clubhouse and went into the tournament headquarters room. I knew she'd be there, but she wasn't. Where was my human?

I hid under the table and wouldn't come out until I saw my human again. I could hear people talking about her saying they hoped she would be alright. I was nervous.

It was hours before I heard her voice, but it was her voice and I ran out from under the table. I froze. It was her voice, but it didn't look like her. You couldn't see one of her eyes—where had it gone? The other eye and her face were black and blue and puffy. Her face looked like one of those Halloween posters. Her hand was in a cast and she looked tired and pale, except for the black, blue, purple and red colors on her face and neck.

As she sat down in a chair, I wandered closer to her. I hoped she wasn't going to die, but she probably wouldn't be at the tournament if she was near death.

We had a tough time adjusting, okay, I had a tough time. She could walk. Apparently, nothing was wrong with her legs other than some bruises, but she wouldn't walk far enough to take me to my favorite places. She also wouldn't drive me anywhere.

Every few days, she went somewhere with Toni, our neighbor and they never took me. I wasn't sure each time that she would come back. She tried to explain about going to a hospital, seeing doctors and surgery. I did know about surgery, but I was always fine the next day. Hopefully, humans could recover as quickly as dogs do.

She was talking funny and I couldn't understand her. But, I did understand that all my training had gone down the tubes, no matter what she was trying to say. Her lips didn't move when she talked and she seldom ate anything, so I didn't get to beg for anything she might be eating.

The only way I got to do anything was if Toni took us both for a short walk. All I had time to do was pee and we were home again. David saved me though. He and his two girls picked us up every afternoon and took us somewhere. Mom didn't walk too far, so I was afraid to leave and go chase rabbits. She might leave without me.

Toni finally took her for some surgery and said Mike would walk me until we returned. I'd had surgery and I was away from home forever. Well, maybe Mike would give me some ice cubes from his glass, but he never did.

Amazingly, my human was home in a couple of hours. She was smiling and talking, and her lips were moving. Toni said she had a broken jaw and they did some kind of new surgery on her. Her mouth wasn't wired shut or anything and she could eat. I liked the sound of that.

My human, who hadn't eaten in a week, cooked some pasta and made a salad. She told me she had been awake during the whole procedure and

Toni had gone in with her and watched. I had no idea what she was talking about; I wanted her to shut up and fix the pasta. I love pasta.

So, she seemed back to normal, almost. She still didn't drive and I was beginning to think life would never be the same again. I used to wash her hands every night, but with that cast on her hand, I couldn't wash her hand. What good would it do to wash just one hand?

I tried to chew the cast off, but she told me no. She knows how much I hate that word, so I got even by not washing the other hand.

Eventually, I got her re-trained, the cast came off, her face returned to normal and she could drive again. But, what if she hadn't come back? I would have to train someone else all over again—or worse—I found out if she died, I'd have to go back to Carson City and be just another one of the whippets.

Dogs can survive the loss of a human and humans can survive the loss of a dog. When my friend, Micki, across the street died, her humans took her out and buried her without much fanfare. She was a great loss to them and I will miss her too, but, it does mean more treats for me. However, humans have a great deal of trouble coping with the loss of another human.

A human dies and even if they didn't know the person who died, they will grieve for the person for years. They take time off work to grieve for dead people like Washington, Lincoln, King, and mourn the loss as though it happened yesterday or that person was one of their best friends.

Their grief is so real, people cannot work, so they take the day off and mourn with millions of other people who didn't know them. If people can't get over their grief there will soon be more days off work for grieving than work days.

Even if they don't take a day off, years after someone dies, they are still grieving. On the anniversary of Elvis' death, thousands of people trek to Graceland.

Someone named Diana was apparently killed in a car accident years ago, and people still cry and build memorials to her. This same grief does not apply to everyone, however. I think you have to be someone who is rich, famous, an entertainer or some other kind of celebrity.

Perhaps what humans need is a grief channel. I'm surprised someone hasn't thought of that; they have a channel for everything else.

Humans could go there and grieve any time they wanted. They wouldn't have to take time off work either. Just pick a name of a dead person and you can grieve, send flowers to a memorial, sign a guest book, offer condolences, or share any thoughts or experiences you had with that person.

You could throw in the names of people you knew and see if others around the country would join in to grieve with you. Humans could grieve forever for anyone.

But, good grief, folks, you have to let go sometime.

Andrew - War

As a dog, I've never quite understood the need for wars. Humans are always at war, either with another country, many other countries, a neighbor, family members and sometimes even with some guy driving down the street.

What do wars accomplish? I guess they help keep the world from being overpopulated, but that hasn't stopped humans from over breeding.

Humans are selfish, looking inward all the time instead of looking outward at the broader aspects of life. Oh, many of the reasons sound honorable and as though humans are looking out for others, but in reality, the reasons are merely excuses.

We want your oil, we want your water, we want your gold, and we want to preserve our freedom. You never hear more important reasons like we want your dogs or you have too many cats—thank goodness.

Usually, I hear humans go to war to protect themselves from bad people and bad ideologies (heard that word on TV). But, who decides who the bad people are? And, is an ideology bad just because it's different?

It looks as though unless all humans can agree on something, one or more humans will fight them over the issue.

Humans fight to resolve the issue at hand, but the wars never end and humans never really feel safe. Every time they end a war, they have to start a new one over the same or a new issue. I guess it's good for the economy. It keeps a lot of people employed, weapons builders, soldiers, medical facility and staffs, undertakers, and on and on.

There always are more humans willing to go, fight and kill or be killed.

What about mini wars? Human wars are not always on a grand scale. There is war in our streets, young people killing each other to prove their worth to a gang; neighbors killing each other because of a barking dog. Students go on killing rampages, workers flip out and attack co-workers, and nothing ever seems to get settled.

Just when you think you might be safe, someone comes and blows airplanes through big buildings and kills thousands. That pissed me off when I heard it because there was no reason to kill those people; they had done nothing wrong.

Of course humans could not let that go; something had to be done. They had been attacked in their own back yard. Even I can understand.

Another war began, but who was it designed to hit? One guy named Saddam something was declared the villainous target, but they got him and now he's dead and the war keeps moving on, moving from country to country because they still can't find who they think is responsible.

A guy named Bin-Laden is the next target. He keeps moving and leaving no forwarding address, so no one can find him after years and years of searching. I think that is kind of funny because with all our technology, satellites can find anything. Heck, they could find me desecrating a fire hydrant before I could even finish.

If humans are trying to control the population of the world by going to war and killing thousands, perhaps they might consider spaying and neutering. It doesn't hurt as much as getting shot and they say it makes you less aggressive afterwards.

If humans are at war because someone has more oil than they do, why not use something else in their gas tanks? I hear they are doing wonderful things with corn.

Do humans fight just because they don't agree with one another? You bet they do and the disagreements are often so trivial. They disagree about religion, politics, abortion, race and all sorts of issues. They can't understand that no one is right and no one is wrong—they just disagree— they don't have to kill each other over it.

Perhaps the entire world needs some therapy to learn how to take care of yourself and let the other person do the same. Boy, that will never happen. They'd just start fighting over who has the best therapist or something.

Humans practice and learn how to kill long before they do it, so that should make war and the killing of any human, premeditated murder.

They sit in front of their television sets and blow away animated enemies all the time. They form teams and play to annihilate each other's team

At one time or another, every human will find himself or herself in a game of war. It permeates their very existence. Hopefully, it will be a small war where no one gets hurt and it ends quickly. Long, drawn-out wars escalate ill feelings and anger, affecting humans their entire lives.

Even my human has a gun in the house, and it's loaded. I've seen some of the target sheets she brought home from the shooting range. I think she's pretty good. She says she will only shoot to defend herself or me.

Susan died before we had to make a decision about shooting someone to defend her.

Our gun, I'm told, will not be used on any animals. I wonder if she would have shot that bear if I hadn't run him off.

Rita - War

WAR HAS TO BE THE stupidest game ever invented; it must have been thought up by men. No woman in her right mind would think blowing away human after human was fun and character building.

Name one woman who would send thousands of men, brothers, sons, husbands, cousins, nephews and nieces off to some foreign land to get killed. Okay, so there may be a couple who would do it, but they don't have the power anyway because it's still a man's war.

When I heard not too long ago, that the president was sending 30,000 more troops clear across the world to be slaughtered, I was outraged. Think of all the families who will lose loved ones—again.

Instead of being critical of human actions, I decided to take a look at this war thing and see if I could come up with a sensible, more logical solution to this war issue.

I know humans could come up with something if they just put their minds to it, but since they aren't trying, here's my solution for ending wars.

Don't send 30,000 more humans. Send 30,000 pit bulls. Once you have them in place, give them the scent of the enemy and turn them loose. They could clear up the whole mess in a week. And, what if we lost some pit bulls in the process—who cares—they aren't whippets. However, my money would be on the pit bulls.

Want to know why the pit bulls would win? They don't play by the rules. Who was the idiot who invented rules for war? It's absurd!

If you are trying to protect yourself, your way of life, your freedoms, you do whatever it takes. There are no rules. Like my mom says, "If someone tries to rape me, he's dead. I'll do whatever it takes to protect myself."

Besides, I don't know if some people are unaware that there are rules in war, or if they don't care. Not everyone plays by the same rules, so how can you have a fair contest?

Who makes up the rules of war? Is there a committee of humans who decide what the rules will be? And, which humans get to be on the committee? How do they get the word out to all humans about the rules? Are there ever any exceptions to the rules? If so, how do you explain them? What are the penalties for breaking the rules and do those penalties apply to all wars?

One side will punish their own war participants if they kill even one civilian.

The other side celebrates if they can fly airplanes into civilian buildings and kill thousands.

One side punishes its humans if they perform any acts which might be construed as torture.

The other side videotapes its torture proceedings and shows it to the world. Then, they decapitate what's left of the human and toss him in the street.

Safe zones are laid out in war zones, but only one side is penalized if they fly into that zone, be it accidental or on purpose. If the other side flies into the zone, it is usually with the intent of destroying that zone and nothing happens to them. There is no such thing as a safe zone in any war.

I know some humans try to think of themselves as humanitarians and it would be wonderful if all humans would do that, but in a war, there are no rules, it's every person for themselves and being nice guys in war never spells victory.

Both sides draw lines in the sand as they say, to define what they are protecting, but those lines are usually so far apart, I wonder why they even try to explain their actions. Just shoot, and last man standing wins.

Don't get me wrong about rules. I think rules are good for many things in life, but it seems like there's always people who do not follow the rules. I mean, why set up rules for marriage, like one man and one woman? One of them is always going to break that rule.

Golf is a kind of war game where everyone is out for him or herself and trying to win. It usually isn't a bloody war; so many humans find it boring. But, in golf, they have rules and everyone must play by the same rules. What a novel idea!

Apparently, the rules are there to protect the field—apparently not much different than what war is all about. Instead of getting killed, or having to die for one reason or another, if someone does something wrong, they get penalized.

If they do something terribly wrong, or keep doing the same things wrong, they don't get to play anymore. Maybe we should try kicking some humans out of the war game if they can't play nice.

Andrew - Rules

HUMANS HAVE RULES FOR EVERYTHING. Some of them are called laws, in fact, most of them are called laws and they govern every aspect of their lives. What they do with those laws and how they abuse them is a matter of public record.

Personally, I'm not that concerned about their laws because I have absolutely no say and no control over them.

It does concern me, however, that they have the audacity to pass laws about dogs, without ever once taking into consideration how it affects the dogs.

I love the signs you see when you're out walking that say you must pick up dog waste—"It's The Law!" The same signs usually say to pick up after your dog. Does that mean they expect dogs to pick up first and humans to do it afterwards?

Dogs must be on a leash at all times, except for specific areas where they are allowed to run free and off leash. And, there's an exception to that also. You can obtain a special permit to have your dog off leash if he's in training, or under complete voice control.

Funny, I never see any signs about picking up after your humans. I've seen men relieving themselves behind trees when they think you aren't watching. This happens a lot on golf courses. I've ridden with my mom enough times to see it happen.

Humans throw waste all over the place and while there is a law against littering, I never see anyone get in trouble for that.

Many humans need to be kept on a leash or maybe one of those ankle bracelets that tracks their every move. It would be much easier to stop them from breaking the rules.

There are many places where you see signs to keep your dogs out of swimming pools. I agree, what dog in his right mind wants to get into a pool where the kids and adults alike have taken a pee?

Dogs go to obedience school to learn the rules of how to get along in the human world. I'd love to see a school for humans where they learn how to get along in a dog's world.

One time, I was running in a field, looking for rabbits, but mostly, I just needed to get out and stretch my legs. Whippets need a lot of exercise. Most dog parks do not give me the room I need. Plus, there's always some mutt around who challenges you to outrun them. Good luck outrunning a whippet.

Anyway, a policeman was driving down the road on the other side of the field where I was running. He stopped my human and told her I had to be on a leash. I'd like to see any human keep up with me even when I'm on a leash.

Of course, I didn't say anything, but the thought occurred to me that there must be something more important for that officer to be doing. I wasn't bothering anyone; no one was even close by. If my mom and I were really guilty of something, wouldn't it have been trespassing or something more important?

A law that is missing is one that would prohibit dogs from humping one another. There was a female German shepherd at this park we used to go that was always trying to hump me. She'd grab me and dig her claws into my belly while she humped.

My mom was angry because that dog's human would not stop her dog—she said it was only natural. It's natural for a female to hump a male? She needed to be spayed, I guess.

I got a serious infection from that dog clawing me and mom tried to get the dogs human to pay for the vet bills. Their friends had to hold the two humans back. There was a lot of shouting and name calling going on.

We decided not to go back to that park again. When a dog misbehaves, I feel like it's the human's fault. Dogs will behave if you let them know what they can and can't do. Sure wish you could get humans to behave as easily.

We later heard that the German shepherd turned on its human one day and caused some serious bodily injury. The human probably deserved it, but the dog was the one that was put down. I'm glad I didn't get stuck with a human like that.

Mom is into rules a lot, but mostly golf rules. She says you can judge humans by how well they follow the rules in golf. If they cheat in golf, they will cheat in life. If they lie or fudge a little in their game, they will do it in life also. If winning is more important to them than following the rules, that's how they will conduct business.

My grandpa once told mom not to do any business with a person who didn't know the rules of golf. He didn't mean you had to know all the rules because no one can do that, but if he didn't know the basic ones, he didn't know basic rules of life.

I've watched a lot of golf in my time, on TV and from a golf cart riding around with mom. One of the things that has always struck me as strange, was there were no referees or umpires.

Oh, sure, mom was a rules official, but from what I could tell, she was there to help people understand the rules and to keep them from doing something wrong before they got penalized.

Perhaps the most awesome thing about golf and all its rules is that players will call penalties on themselves if they do something wrong. Can you imagine a basketball player calling a foul on himself?

A good example happened at one of the tournaments my mom was officiating. After the round, a player was preparing to turn in her scorecard and said she thought she had done something wrong in the playing of one hole.

Apparently, she had tried to play a ball out of a water hazard, hit it further into the hazard, and not knowing where to drop it, dropped it from a point across from where she thought it landed on the second hit.

When it was determined that the place she dropped the ball was the wrong place, she would receive a two-stroke penalty, but when asked if she had gained a significant advantage from where she should have dropped it, she said, "Hell, yeah. I was fifty yards closer and didn't have to go over the water."

Needless to say, under the rules of golf, she was disqualified. No one would have known if she hadn't reported her actions to the rules committee.

The player laughed and said, "Well, I guess the twelve strokes I took on that hole wouldn't have helped me win anyway."

Do you know that some areas have rules about how many dogs you can have? Supposedly, where I live, you can only have one dog. That's fine with me—I'm not keen on sharing my human with another dog.

Some places also restrict the kinds of dogs you can have. Pit bulls are not allowed in some areas. That doesn't bother me because I'm scared to death of them.

There are rules regarding dogs who bark too much and some of them have had their barkers cut out and can't bark any more. I hate to see that. Getting a sports collar or some other gadget will break them of that habit if you spend enough time with them.

Other places regulate the size dog you can have. I would think size shouldn't matter. How well the dog behaves should be more important. One place I know of restricts the size of dogs to basically the same size as cats. How rude is that?

Speaking of cats, how come they don't have the same rules as we do? Those damn fur balls can do their business anywhere and no one picks up after them. They come and go as they please without leashes.

There are no neutering and spaying rules for them and they are always propagating like crazy. It must be because dogs are man's best friend and must follow man's rules, while cats are just a pain in the butt.

Rita - Rules

I HATE RULES OF ANY kind. I get along just fine without them. They usually don't make any sense and they interfere with my freedoms.

Humans have so many rules and all their rules have exceptions to the rule; it will make your head spin.

My human talks a lot about the rules of golf. Have you ever read them, or tried to read them? They truly are the most confusing rules I've ever read.

Let me give you an example: Rule 16-1 simply states, "The line of putt must not be touched. That makes sense to me and would be so easy to follow, IF they didn't add the word "except".

What follows are seven exceptions to that one statement. Turns out the line of putt can be touched if you are removing a moveable obstruction (look up moveable obstruction), if you are repairing an old hole plug or ball marks, if you are pressing down a ball marker, if you are lifting or replacing the ball, if you are measuring, if you are removing loose impediments, and a player may place the club in front of the ball when addressing it. Otherwise, the line of putt must not be touched.

Wouldn't it have been simpler to say you may touch the line of putt when you do these things, otherwise you can't?

Don't get me wrong, the rules of golf are wonderful guidelines for playing the game, and are so thorough, there is no need for referees or umpires, provided the humans are honest. They could be wonderful guidelines for people to follow in their lives, if they were changed slightly.

Did you know there are only 34 rules in the rules of golf? It's true. The problem is, with all the exceptions to each rule, there are umpteen decisions to consider before making a ruling.

Life doesn't need all those decisions if we simplify the 34 original rules.

Rule No. 1 – The Game

The purpose of the game is to get from Point A to Point B. You must not do anything to influence the outcome if it gives you a significant advantage over another human.

You must not waive any of the rules of golf as this would be cheating and cheating is not allowed in life.

Finally, if something is not covered in the rules, humans should base their decisions in accordance with equity for all.

Rule No. 2 –Match Play

This rule is probably not needed. No one should play with matches, especially dogs because if they started a fire, they have no way of putting it out. Peeing will not work.

Rule No. 3 – Stroke Play

What a delightful rule this is. Humans would be wise to follow this rule where dogs are concerned or where loved ones are concerned. You can keep score of how many strokes you get or how many you hand out. The total won't matter because the more strokes you give your pets and fellow human beings, the better everyone will feel. There is a provision for doubt as to how to proceed. If you are not sure of how to stroke, you try a second method and see if that works.

If a human refuses to comply with a rule affecting the rights of another human, he/she is disqualified. (See definition of disqualification at the end of the rules)

Rule No. 4 – Clubs

All humans are allowed to have clubs, but they need to conform so all humans have access to the same kind of clubs.

If your club becomes damaged, it may be repaired or in some cases, replaced. In any case, a human must not have more than fourteen clubs in their lifetime. It would just be too time consuming.

Rule No. 5 – The Ball
I think I would eliminate this rule. It obviously was someone's attempt to metaphorically relate a ball to the circle of life; kind of like take the ball and run with it. Most humans wouldn't grasp this kind of philosophy, so why confuse them?

Rule No. 6 – The Player
This is probably one of the most important rules in life because it directly concerns every human. The rule has many provisions for those who are handicapped. It gives them a slight edge at various points in their life over those who do not need as much help.
No one with a handicap is ever looked down upon or treated any differently than one without a handicap and it allows for everyone to participate equally in the game of life.

Rule No. 7 – Practice
Everyone is allowed to practice before heading on to the next phase of their life

Rule No. 8 – Advice
You must not give erroneous advice to anyone and you must not give advice that would give one human a significant advantage over another human.

Rule No. 9 – Information as to Strokes Taken
It is important for everyone to know how many strokes each other has. (See Rule 3) If one human has too many strokes, adjustments should be made so that everyone plays equally when it comes to getting strokes. You must not give wrong information; that is called lying and is not allowed.

Rule No. 10 – Order of Play
How you play the game of life depends on which avenue you are pursuing. The order should be determined by who arrived first, who has the right-of-way, or who has the farthest to go to reach their destination. There is no penalty if you mistakenly play out of turn, but if you do it to give another human an advantage, you can be disqualified. Disqualification in the game of life should be taken very seriously. I don't think you want to know what happens

to those who are disqualified. (See the definition of disqualification at the end of the rules.)

Rule No. 11 – Teeing Ground
This is another rule to eliminate. No one should be allowed to be teed off on a routine basis; everyone stay calm.

Rule No. 12 – Searching for and Identifying Ball
This rule can only be used if a human has accepted the premise that the ball represents life. (See Rule 5) Humans can search for their path through life, but they cannot take too much time. If they take too much time, they should abandon their first attempt and try again.
Humans are allowed to lose their life's path (the ball) as many times as is needed in order to attain their ultimate goal. They should stay on their own path and not use another human's path.

Rule No. 13 – Ball Played as It Lies
This one is confusing enough in golf, why drag it over into real life. Most humans don't correlate the ball with life anyway, and those who do probably think it's okay to improve your lie.

Rule No. 14 - Striking the Ball
You must not strike out at life or each other, and if you need to, it must be done fairly. Pushing, scraping and spooning are not allowed. Also, you may not use artificial devices to strike at anything.

Rule No. 15 – Substituted Ball; Wrong Ball
These are very serious infractions. You cannot substitute someone's life for your own; it's called identity theft. You will rot in jail if you try to play out someone else's life. If you can't find your own, start over.

Rule No. 16 – The Putting Green
I really know of nothing in life that correlates exactly to a putting green. There may be two explanations. One is that as humans succeed at each stage of their life, they will hear that wonderful sound of a ball dropping into the hole; kind of the cha-ching in

life. If you've never heard the sound of a ball dropping into the hole, go to the practice putting green and hit a ball until one drops in; you'll know what I mean.

The second explanation is that when you take that final stroke in life, your ball will disappear in the hole, the sound of it dropping will not even be heard and you'll be outta here.

Rule 17 – The Flagstick

Everyone knows what a flagstick is; it marks a significant achievement in your life. You can have help reaching your flagstick, but if that help is not authorized by you, the person who infringed on your goal of reaching the flagstick, will be penalized. Humans just cannot interfere with one another.

Rule 18 – Ball at Rest Moved

Perhaps we will need to change some of the titles of our rules of life, but for now, we're following the ones from golf. Obviously, if your life has come to rest and someone moves it, they are grave robbers or family members in dispute over what you left each of them. I don't think we even have to mention this, but it is important in golf, and if someone would move your ball at rest during a round of golf, imagine what they would do to you after your life has come to rest.

Rule 19 – Ball in Motion Deflected or Stopped

If your life, while it is moving forward, gets accidently derailed, deflected or stopped by any outside agency, it is a rub of the green, there is no penalty and you must continue with your life at the spot it came to rest.

Rule 20 – Lifting, Dropping and Placing; Playing from Wrong Place

Sometimes, there will be storms which come into your life and make it almost impossible to move ahead with your life. Under special circumstances, you will be allowed to lift and drop or place your life where it will allow you to move forward.

Cleaning up the pieces of your life will also be an option at times.

However, if you take advantage of this rule and continue your life from a place where you are not allowed, and you have committed a serious offense or obtained a significant advantage, you must correct your error. Failure to do so will result in disqualification. Be sure to check later to find out exactly what disqualification means.

Rule 21 – Cleaning Ball
You cannot stop and clean up your life any time you wish. However, this rule does allow, under certain circumstances, to clean up the mess you have made of your life; it is called bankruptcy.

Rule 22 – Ball Assisting or Interfering with Play
If your life assists or interferes with another humans ability to play the game of life, call a time out, pick up your life and put it on hold until the other person is out of your way. During your time out, you may not clean up your own life.

Rule 23 – Loose impediments
Loose impediments are natural things that God and Mother Nature put in your way to see how you handle different situations. It's kind of a little joke they play on you. Except when you are in one of life's hazards, pick them up and throw them away.
If you are in a hazard, you must not touch these loose impediments because obviously, you have done something wrong, or you wouldn't be there. If you can somehow manage to get out of the hazard and continue with your life, without touching a loose impediment, you have passed another of Mother Nature's little tests.

Rule 24 – Obstructions
An obstruction is anything artificial or man-made. You are entitled to free relief from both movable and immovable obstructions. It's obvious that someone is trying to mess with your game and cause you to fall behind while they surge forward.

Rule 25 – Abnormal Ground Conditions, Embedded Ball and Wrong Putting Green
In life, there are numerous abnormal ground conditions. Everyone must expect some problems as they go through life, but

occasionally an abnormal condition arises, such as casual water (flooding), ground under repair (construction) cast or runway on the course.

The cast could be any kind of a cast on a humans leg, arm, whatever, and the runway, of course refers to airports. You are allowed relief in all these situations.

If your life becomes embedded in its own way, you are allowed to lift, clean and drop it back into play near the spot where it became embedded.

The wrong putting green presents some problems. While everyone knows the putting green represents the end of one's life, especially on the last hole of your round, avoiding the end by playing to a wrong green does not circumvent the inevitable.

You must take relief from the wrong putting green and get back to where you belong and finish the game. Failure to do so results in disqualification. Check further for details on disqualification.

Rule 26 – Water Hazards (Including Lateral Water Hazards)
Listen up, now, this is one of the most important rules in life. There are tons of hazards in everyone's life. Getting through or around them is one of life's biggest challenges. If you play smart, don't let your ego get the best of you, ignore the constant peer pressures put upon you, and know your own game, hazards will never come into play.

However, humans are not known for being able to do any of the above, so they must deal with hazards. There is almost always a penalty for being in a hazard and trying to avoid such a penalty by blasting one's way out of it, is not a good idea.

Recently, I was watching a golf tournament and a player tried to hit her way out of a hazard when she clearly should have taken a penalty and just continued on her way. She did hit the ball and it landed a few yards outside the hazard. Meantime, she was leaning on her club in the hazard and watched the ball roll back into the hazard. You cannot ground your club in a hazard when your ball is in it. She ended up with twice the penalty she would have incurred if she had just played smart.

Oh, a quick side note here. The player argued with the committee that made the decision on the penalty. You'll see why this is not a good idea when you get to Rules 33 and 34.

Rule 27 – Ball Lost or Out of Bounds; Provisional Ball
If your life becomes lost, you certainly have to start over; the same applies if you somehow go out of bounds. However, you are allowed to play provisionally. Basically, even though all these actions involve a penalty, hitting provisionally before going forward, not knowing where your life is, saves you time and stress. This is called therapy.

Rule 28 – Ball Unplayable
How many times do humans find themselves in situations where their life just cannot proceed further because of the spot they find themselves in?
This rule allows you, with a small penalty (because you shouldn't have allowed yourself to get into that situation) to get out of a jam and move on.
Humans often overlook the power of this rule which allows them to move on without horrendous stress issues or multiple strokes and penalties.

Rules 29-32 involve different forms of play which I will not discuss because I think they are kind of kinky and depend on others to play instead of life being played by each person. They are some sort of sex game like threesomes and foursomes.

Rule 33 – The Committee
Now, we come to the meat of all these rules. If humans must play by rules, they must have a committee to govern them and make decisions on how they play the game of life.
This committee is all powerful and their decisions are final and binding.
You must have a strong leader to head this group, and since the committee is to govern all humans, it would not be fair to place a human in charge. It would be like putting a fox in the hen house to guard the chickens.
The next best solution is to put man's best friend in charge. After all, who knows humans better than their dogs?
If you have been following this logic at all, I'm sure you know who would be the best choice to head up the committee.

I graciously accept the position and invite any dogs who would like to help govern humans in their lives to contact me through my human's web page. www.luckiiludwig.com
Trust me, I WILL get the message—she is well trained.

And, Finally, Rule 34 – Disputes and Decisions
What disputes?

Disqualification only comes into play in extreme cases of abuse and total disregard for the rules of life. The penalty is death!

Andrew - Holidays

HOLIDAYS ARE WONDERFUL TIMES FOR humans, probably because they get to take time off from work and have a good reason to get drunk.

For dogs, well, we really don't need holidays because we don't work and we don't usually drink too much, and if we did, we wouldn't need a holiday to do it on.

I almost got drunk one time. My mom and I were camping out in the middle of this lake, away from roads, marinas and people. We seldom saw people where we were.

One time we hiked around to the other side of the cove where we were camped, and we spotted another couple. All of us were amazed to see other humans in this location. They invited us to join them, so we did.

They were celebrating an anniversary of some sort and offered my mom a glass of wine. They offered me nothing.

As they were all talking, I noticed that when they sat their glasses of wine down, they were on little tables next to their chairs and it put the glasses right at my level.

Naturally, I assumed they did this so I could also participate in the celebration. I wasn't sure I liked the taste of the wine, so I moved from one human to the next, sampling all the wine.

When I got to the only man in the group, I took a taste of what I thought was wine. I found out later he was drinking beer. Now, this was something I could get my teeth into.

No one had noticed my drinking from their wine glasses. I was discreet and didn't empty the glasses, but when I got to the beer, I couldn't help myself and drained it.

That was my downfall. When the man discovered his glass was empty, they all figured it out; so much for my celebrating.

Dogs love a lot of the human holidays. For one thing, if the humans are off work, it often means more attention from them and longer walks throughout the day.

Thanksgiving is a great time. We either get to go for a ride to someone's house or we stay home and lots of people come to our house. Either way, there's usually an extra dog or two to play with.

The house smells great. I learned early on that my mom fixes a turkey. I love turkey and we don't have it too often. It makes both mom and me fart. She thinks mine smell worse.

Once the turkey really gets going in that oven, I like to position myself on the floor underneath the door that will eventually open and spit out the turkey. I want to be first.

For some reason, when I sit there, people are always yelling at me about being in the way. How could I possibly be in the way when I was there first? They laugh and move around me. Thanksgiving seems to be a jovial time for humans.

Thanksgiving lasts more than one day—at least the food does. I prefer the turkey, but I've snuck dressing, gravy, potatoes and rolls when no one was looking. I can do without those red berry things and the sweet potatoes.

When they put out those plates with all the snack things on them, the plate goes at the end of a table and I'm able to get a paw on many things without anyone seeing me. I love the carrots and the olives. Don't care too much for celery but will eat it if that's all that's left or if it has peanut butter or cheese on it. And, I haven't met a pickle I like.

I heard mom say once not to put any green onions on the plate because they aren't good for dogs. I guess she knows I get into that stuff.

There are two holidays we dogs hate; New Year's Eve and Fourth of July.

First of all, what is so special about starting a new year? Seems to me it is just another day, but since humans love to party and drink too much, I guess the new day of a new year is as good a reason as any.

Imagine if they celebrated the New Year in a dog's life how many parties they could throw in one of their years?

The start of a new year apparently brings out something in humans you don't see on other holidays. For some reason, that is the time when they grab their guns and shoot into the air. Why would they want to shoot air? Air never hurt anyone unless that air was so polluted already by humans.

Dogs hate the sound of gunfire. That's the time to run and hide under the bed, or better yet, under the covers and hope your mom is hiding there too.

Humans spend lots of money on decorations, cheap champagne and trinkets they can only use once because they put a date on them and that date only happens once in a lifetime.

I had to laugh when there was a big deal made over the year 2000. Humans were not only celebrating a new year, a new decade, but a new millennium like they had lived through it all. I guess they could be given a little slack because they sure won't see another one thousand years.

Maybe they should have taken a look back at all those years and tried to learn something from it all.

Of course, there's always the fireworks. I have no idea how much money is spent on them. They shoot so many you can barely see them from all the smoke they create, but, by then they are probably too drunk to appreciate them.

Fireworks are another reason for dogs to hide; they make too much noise. Some dogs howl these mournful cries when the fireworks go off. I always thought it was a waste of time because no one can hear you and if they could, they wouldn't stop shooting fireworks.

One of my friends, Koki, goes bananas and tears her apartment up. Sometimes, she has to go sit in the car to calm down.

People, who care about what we go through, give us this stuff called Rescue Remedy. I don't know what's in it, but it helps calm our nerves; works great on humans too.

Fourth of July, what is it? I know, it's Independence Day, the fourth day in the month of July. It comes in the middle of summer after a long spell of not having any holidays and it will be a long time before they get another holiday.

Most of them have taken off work for weeks at a time during the summer, why do they need another holiday?

Independence from what? Humans are no more independent than they were when they were born. They are dependent on so many things, like drugs, each other, their families, their jobs, all the gods they worship, the things they worry about—the list goes on and on.

This celebration, like New Years, also carries a multitude of fireworks and noise. Fireworks manufacturers must make a ton of money and they only have to work hard twice a year.

If humans knew how to safely set off fireworks, they could do it themselves, and many try. What fools they are. Every year, many lose their fingers, arms, their lives and their homes from the fires these things spurn. I pity the poor innocent people whose homes burn to the ground because of someone else's negligence and stupidity.

Some of the holidays make no sense to me. Take Memorial Day, for instance. Those who have died are to be remembered on that day and it can only be done if you take the day off work.

If the people are so important that they need to be remembered, why not remember them all year long?

Of course, they follow this up with a day to remember just the veterans, another day off work. These heroes should be remembered more than just one day a year.

Why not a day to remember all those who have been killed by drunk drivers, or a day to remember those who have died because of domestic violence. Humans could come up with a lot more holidays if they put their minds to it.

One of the funniest holidays is Labor Day—like they've been working so hard all year long without a holiday? It makes no sense to me.

There are two really fun holidays but humans don't take the day off work. Halloween is fun because you can dress up any way you want, look stupid and everyone loves it.

At my house, people don't come trick-or-treating; their dogs come. Some of the dogs dress up and look so cute. Mom takes pictures of them and gives them jerky treats. The humans then gather at someone's house for drinks.

We don't pull tricks on each other, though I once thought it would be a good trick to take all the fire hydrants in our park and put them all in one place. That way, dogs wouldn't have to search all over for them.

The other fun holiday is Valentine's Day. It's a time to remember someone you love and give them special treats. I always wanted a box of chocolates, but never got any.

My mom got a box one year and she and her friends seemed to really enjoy the chocolate. When she went out to dinner with some friends, I climbed up on the counter and knocked the box down on the floor.

It opened and there were all kinds of treats in there. I took a bite out of one of the chocolates, but before I finished it, I knew I was going to be in trouble. It would be doggie prison time again. I didn't know what to do. I thought about hiding the box and everything, but I knew she'd miss it.

I left the box on the floor and the half- eaten piece of chocolate next to it. Maybe I would only be half in trouble and my prison sentence would be half as long.

The hard part was not eating the rest of the piece of chocolate. I sat and looked at it a long time. It had tasted so good. It was all I could do to just leave it there.

Mom laughed when she got home and found the box on the floor. She knew exactly how many pieces had been in that box, so she knew I only tasted one piece. She was so proud of me I didn't have to go to prison.

Apparently, had I eaten the whole box, I probably would have gone to the vet again, so I'm glad I didn't go any farther.

She took some hamburger and made a heart shaped treat out of it for me. It was even better than the chocolate and I didn't get in trouble. How wonderful it is to be loved.

Two holidays that are special for many humans that dogs truly enjoy, are Christmas and Easter.

At Christmas, we put a tree up in our house. The first year, I was about six months old and I was thrilled with having a tree in the house. It was cold and wet outside and I didn't like being cold and wet, so having a tree in the nice warm living room was like a dream come true. After all, Susan had indoor facilities.

But, as soon as the tree went up, mom put this white, fluffy stuff around the base of the tree. She called it snow. Susan immediately went into the snow and rearranged it, making a sweet little bed for herself. I was surprised.

Susan gave me her two evil eyes look and let it be known that it was her tree and I was, under no circumstances, to come near it. My hopes for an indoor place to relieve myself disappeared. Well, Susan had been there longer than I had, so she was pretty set in her own traditions.

Mom always hung stockings for us and put treats in them. After Susan died, she still hung one for her, but it was always empty.

One morning we got up and the white snow stuff was all messed up and pushed into a little bed like Susan used to do. Mom thought I did it and cried because it reminded her of Susan. But, I hadn't touched it. I think Susan's spirit returned and did it.

I never went near a Christmas tree again.

The other wonderful holiday is Easter. It is really part of the Christmas holiday for some, although humans don't go all out with presents and tons of decorations. I think they are still paying off the bills from Christmas.

Apparently, someone special was born on Christmas and died on Easter. Mom says humans go to church more on Easter Sunday than any other day of the year. Guess that is one of those mourning things they do.

Mom would get me up before the sun came up on Easter Sunday and make me go out and do my business. I'd get breakfast and go back to bed while she went to sunrise services.

She had to go real early so we could be ready for the part of Easter that dogs like the most—the annual Easter rabbit hunt.

A bunch of us would meet at Wilson Park and chase rabbits. Some of the humans had children and they would hunt eggs. I have no idea where those eggs came from because rabbits and squirrels don't lay eggs; at least I never saw any at the park.

The adults would help the kids because they always seemed to know where to find the eggs. They certainly didn't need to help the dogs, and we were free to run all we wanted. Children needed to be kept in tow, but not us.

Sometimes we would go to a human's house after the hunt so the humans could eat. Most of us were too tired to eat, but we would get special snacks. They were good, but I know we didn't get anything like what the humans got and their food always smelled better than ours.

I have always been amazed at how many holidays these people come up with and wondered why they thought of so many. I guess their lives are pretty dull so they have to think of reasons to have fun.

At least they try to plan activities for the dogs on some of those days.

Rita — Holidays

Holidays, Holidays, Holidays—that's all humans think about. They have a holiday for everything and a reason to take more days off work than they actually work. On top of that, they have vacations too. I don't think they really like to work; they'd rather party and celebrate some ridiculous event most of them know nothing about.

Did you know they even have a holiday to celebrate my human's birthday? It's true; Cinco de Mayo. And, it's all because she was born on that day, hundreds of years ago (in dog years).

I was born on Aug. 24, but there isn't a holiday to celebrate my birth. Aren't I important? Well, of course I am, so next year, everyone take that day off work and get drunk.

My human is silly about her birthday. There are all these ads out about "Are you ready for Cinco de Mayo?" She always stands up and yells at the ads, "Of course I'm ready."

Humans—they are so childish. The only good thing about the day is the margaritas. A margarita is something you put in a glass and drink, and if you think about it, part of that drink is named after me. Maybe they should serve them on my birthday.

I do enjoy my human's birthday. All those margaritas have ice cubes in them and I love ice cubes. Humans love to watch me eat them because I do it with fervor, passion and because they taste so good.

Our neighbors, Mike and Toni, make the best margaritas and Mike always gives me ice cubes from his glass. They taste so much better than ones out of the freezer. A few of those cubes and I don't care whose birthday we celebrate.

Most humans say they love to celebrate birthdays, but then they complain about how old they've gotten. What fun is that? Of course, if it's someone else's birthday, they make fun of how old that person is.

Seems to me if a birthday is something special to a person, they should just have fun with it and be happy. My human doesn't care how old she is on her birthday, she's happy to be having another one. At her age, I guess it doesn't matter anyway.

The park we live in is full of old people, so on someone's birthday, you have to sit and listen to all the things that ail them. I'd do it on another day or not at all.

Some humans are so old; they can't remember how old they are. They also can't remember what they did yesterday or what they had for breakfast.

What difference does it make how old you are? My human says I'll be seven on my next birthday. Is that supposed to mean something? In dog years, I'll be a lot older than seven. In fact, when I'm ten, my human says she and I will be the same age; does that make any sense?

Ever heard of George Washington, Abraham Lincoln, Martin Luther King? Humans celebrate their birthdays, but how many really knew them?

I'm surprised humans don't celebrate every day of the year because someone was born on that day and it doesn't matter if you knew them or not—just celebrate. But, humans tend to think some people are more important than they are.

I hate some of the holidays, especially the ones that don't involve me. New Years and Fourth of July come to mind.

On New Years, humans all over the planet celebrate and they put all those celebrations on television because for some reason, they don't all celebrate at the same time.

You see the celebrations in Australia, China, Russia, London, you name it, and someone is celebrating like one day makes such a huge difference in their lives.

When it comes time to celebrate in the United States, everyone has to watch New York do it, then Chicago, Denver and finally Sacramento. How did Sacramento get tied in with that group? I guess it's because we live in this area.

Even Davis celebrates, and it looks like each place tries to outdo the one before it. Why? They are all the same. Everyone spends way more money than they have to shoot off fireworks and huge light shows.

Humans are always complaining about pollution, destroying the ozone, bad air quality.

Ever see a shot from space on New Year's Eve? Me neither, but I can only imagine seeing this huge cloud of smoke covering the whole planet from these fireworks. Talk about pollution!

The whole planet doesn't do this twice a year, only the United States. Americans pull the same type of celebration in July, about the time the air has finally cleared from New Years.

Once again, millions of dollars are blown up in a matter of minutes and polluting the air all over.

Dogs do not like these celebrations. First, I thought we had a noise ordinance in this town. Too much noise and you get fined. They even tried to fine a woman here for snoring too loudly.

The celebrations are loud and it hurts my ears, not to mention I find it extremely frightening and scary.

Humans try to drug us before the explosions begin to make us calm. Rescue Remedy is a laugh. It's supposed to rescue us from things we find stressful. It helps a little; we are not as stressed out when we're on it, but we still know what's going on and we're nervous.

It's bad enough that Mother Nature has to butt in on occasion and produce loud thunder claps all around us, but I guess she has her reasons. At least she doesn't pollute the air, and I would never argue with Mother Nature; she is the one person who is much better than me.

I don't get as stressed out as some dogs I know. Koki tears up her whole apartment when fireworks or thunder is happening. I pace a lot and then hide under the covers. My human often hides there with me. I guess I'm supposed to protect her.

Human celebrations like New Years and Fourth of July aren't only about the fireworks. It seems these days are also for eating and drinking too much and suffering later.

Why do humans torture themselves by eating too much food, most of which is not good for their bodies, and drinking so much they get sick? Celebrations are supposed to be fun and happy, not something you spend hours bent over the toilet and getting sick.

90

Thank goodness my human doesn't do that—I drink out of that toilet. She does, however, eat things she shouldn't. One time, on her birthday, she went to this great steak house and they had a special on all you can eat ribs. She knows she can't eat more than a few, but, oh no, she had to eat too many, and brought some home so she could do it all over the next day. At least she had the decency to use the spare bathroom.

It appears that every month humans have to celebrate something and take time off work to do it. In February, they celebrate the birthdays of dead presidents. They used to have two different dates they celebrated, but someone got wise and now they lump the presidents into one big weekend.

But, also in February, they have Valentine's Day. It's a cute little day to remember ones you love. Since I'm my human's little valentine, I get special treats, an extra squirrel hunt, but no chocolate.

If people set aside a day to honor loved ones, why do they turn around and beat the crap out of them?

March is another month for humans to get blottoed. Saint Patrick's Day and green beer, plus corned beef and cabbage marks this holiday.

Who was Saint Patrick? I'm not sure saints are allowed to drink green beer or any beer for that matter, but I don't know about the corned beef and cabbage. Somehow, none of it sounds too good to me and I'm a garbage hound. I also like my beer a light amber color, if you don't mind.

I don't drink beer often, but I wish I could. My human is often offered a beer when we visit some of the neighbors. I always sit and beg nicely, unless they don't notice me and then I make a fuss. The good neighbors bring a small bowl to my human and force her to share a few sips.

Personally, I think Saint Patrick was probably a God-fearing man who would have been appalled by public drunkenness.

April seems the month when humans relax and recover from all the celebrating they had been doing. There are no fireworks being shot off during the month that I know of.

After the rest in April, humans go wild in May, starting with my human's birthday on the fifth. Since when does a fifth of booze have to be consumed on the fifth of the month?

This is followed up by a celebration of mothers and is usually a nice quiet Sunday when people behave like their mothers taught them to behave.

My mother Helen lives somewhere in Tennessee or Kentucky. While I am grateful that she gave me life, I haven't seen her in years, but I do think about her on mother's day.

At the end of the month, humans go berserk again with Memorial Day. They also say it marks the beginning of summer which is ridiculous because summer doesn't start until mid-June.

I don't know who they are remembering, but it must be a lot of people based on the amount of alcohol and food they have to consume to honor these people, most of whom I'm told, are dead.

June brings celebrations for people graduating from just about anything—high school, kindergarten, college, junior college, boot camp, beauty school or whatever. They should also celebrate for all of us dogs who graduated from obedience school.

Since May celebrated mothers, June is to celebrate fathers. This is another nice quiet way to honor those who brought you into the world. I never knew my father, but I know my human's father was very special to her.

We already know what happens in July and because of it, humans tend to take August off. I think that's because so many of them are on vacation and it would be hard to get them all together.

Labor Day is in September and all humans need to take a day off from their labors because they have been working so hard all year. Like what a phony excuse for a day off. They say it also marks the end of summer, but their calendars show they celebrate a little early for that.

October is Halloween time. Humans love to be scared out of their wits by monsters, boogey men, and all sorts of hideous creatures, and they love to do this through their children. Heck, kids get scared seeing Santa Claus, imagine what it does when they see someone dressed up like George Bush.

The children are supposed to go trick-or-treating and gather up copious amounts of candy which will ruin their teeth, make them fat and may contain dangerous things put in it by mean ogres.

Plus, if they don't get treats, they are allowed to pull tricks on you, most of which will get them arrested. My human says they used to throw rotten apples and eggs at cars and houses or soap up windows. Those are all acts of vandalism and do carry a fine if caught.

Dogs can come to our house and get jerky treats and they don't have to wear a costume. The ones who do dress up look silly and extremely uncomfortable. I do not have to dress up; I go as I am—a beautiful princess.

Most dogs do not trick if they don't receive a treat. They may mark a human's tire, fire hydrant or bush, however. While this is not a tasteful thing to do, it is not against the law.

November brings Thanksgiving. What a great time to celebrate. Winter is coming and everyone will have to be indoors more than normal and Thanksgiving is held indoors at someone's house with plenty of great food and, oh yes, plenty of drinks.

Every true dog loves turkey. I also love carrots, olives (when I can steal one) potatoes, gravy, dressing and even yams if they are cooked in butter. Unfortunately, I don't get to eat a lot of any of those things, except maybe turkey with a little gravy on it.

I did steal a bit of pumpkin pie one time, but I didn't care for it. I ate it because I had taken the time to steal it. When I go to other dog's houses, I always check their food dishes and the kitchen floor to see if anything is there. I often eat some of the dog food even if I don't like it. I want my friends to know I can do whatever I want when I visit.

Several of my friends are a little annoyed with how I walk in and take charge when I'm in their homes and they have told their humans to pick up all their dishes when I walk in. That is so rude; I would never do that to them when they come into my house. Of course, I would make sure there was nothing in my bowl and I had already cleaned up the kitchen floor.

Christmas is another of those fun winter activities for humans and their dogs. I don't see the need for a lot of decorations, however, because they sometimes interfere with my movements. One time, my human put up this sled with Snoopy at the helm, driving a bunch of Woodstocks. I didn't know she'd done that. She called me to come and see what she'd done. I slid around the corner and ran into the sled, and sent all those yellow birds flying.

I was not impressed with decorations being in my way, but my human laughed and put it all back up again. Thank goodness they were gone after a week or two. I think the birds flew away so I wouldn't hurt them.

Christmas means presents, and I get a ton of them. I like getting new toys, not the kind you play with, the kinds that look good when I place them on my bed to help me stare at my human.

One of the presents I got was a stuffed cookie monster. Man, was he ugly; didn't look anything like a whippet, but they never do. I make sure he is right in front so my human cannot miss his stare.

Since so many humans think I'm wonderful, I receive a lot of gifts, mostly treats because they know how I love them. Unfortunately most of them come in jars or other containers which are not possible to open without the use of a thumb.

However, several treats came in plastic containers with screw caps on the top. These I love because I know how to get tops off plastic containers.

When empty plastic bottles go into the recycling bag, I go through and pull them out. When my human is away, I work at taking the tops off. The empty cranberry bottles are the best. I like cranberry juice and there's always a little in the bottom.

I used to be able to get into the full bottles of water until one time, I opened too many of them and couldn't drink all the water so it went all over the floor. Now the bottles are placed high out of my reach.

But, I digress.

On Christmas day I get to go to one of my favorite hunting grounds. My human calls it my field of dreams, whatever that means. All I know is there are tons of rabbits running every which way and I try to get them all.

We fix good things for Christmas dinner, at least they smell good and my human makes sure there is something I can eat.

Humans celebrate the birth of someone. I always find it strange that humans often give birth to just one child, but apparently this child was super special because he's been dead a long time and they still celebrate his birth.

When I gave birth to my nine pups, I think the breeders celebrated with a bottle of wine. Now all they do is try and keep track of where everyone went when they left home.

I'm always getting reports about where the kids are and what they are doing. I could care less—I did my job, but my human downloads pictures and shows me. They all look alike and since I can't smell them, I can't tell them apart.

I didn't mention the Easter holiday because humans never seem to know when it is. I think it's sometime in March or April. They celebrate the death of the man who was born on Christmas day, but they don't seem to have a fix on what Friday in the spring he died.

Oh well, Easter is for dogs anyway. That's the time we get to do our Easter rabbit hunt. I never have hunted at Wilson Park. Apparently they no longer believe in traditions, so we go to different places each year.

Funny how humans think it is barbaric for dogs to hunt rabbits. They don't seem to have a problem hunting deer, ducks, geese, bears and all sorts of other animals. They even travel to far away countries to hunt "big" game.

Personally, I would be afraid to hunt anything bigger than myself.

There are a few days set aside each year for humans that are not listed as holidays, but they are celebrated in much the same way as the traditional ones.

There's the super bowl, for instance. I can only let my imagination run wild as to what a super bowl is, but I picture the largest dog dish I've ever seen, chucked full of kibble, dog food and chicken. I'd want mostly chicken in my super bowl and I'd eat until I got sick.

Come to think of it, that's what humans do with their super bowl—eat, drink and get sick. Mom says it's not safe to go out on super bowl Sunday because of all the drunks.

One thing really bothers me about the super bowl. Mom says there are more cases of domestic violence on that day than any other single day of the year. I've never understood why any celebration means it's okay to beat up members of your family.

But, when is it ever okay to beat and molest those who are supposedly near and dear to you? Humans have such weird values. They criticize one another all the time when they disagree about anything.

They maul, maim and kill their loved ones when they don't see eye to eye. And, they kill strangers for no reason at all, unless you think just being different or just being there is a reason.

Other non holiday celebrations are the same, like the national championships of any major college sport. The game is over, someone wins and someone loses, why does that give anyone the right to riot, burn, loot, and create mayhem?

The World Series, world soccer finals, the list goes on and on. Humans need to follow some rules of golf that I mentioned earlier and learn how to accept things and get over it.

When I don't like another dog, another human or the situation I'm facing, I ignore them all and stare at my human until she gets out the ice cream and things will be fine.

Andrew - Fishing/Camping

ONE OF THE GREATEST THINGS anyone can do is find something they enjoy and then do it.

For dogs, this is sometimes hard, because they don't know enough things to do. Oh, sure, there's always chasing squirrels and rabbits, going for long walks and getting treats.

I take great pleasure in lying out in the sun and relaxing, especially after a long run. But, I can't go anywhere or do anything without my mom, so how do I learn about other things to do?

I learn from mom because she knows all kinds of things to enjoy and ways to relax and "get away from it all" as she says.

When I was still quite young, she took me fishing and camping. I didn't know how to do either, but I could tell from her expression, it was going to be something very special.

We spent two days packing up things we would need. She had a boat and we were going to pull it along with us behind her truck. We had to put all kinds of things in there and she explained them to me. I had no clue what she was talking about—fishing poles, net, fish finder, downrigger, gas can, battery, life jackets, motor. The list went on and on, never seeming to end and she had to check and double check to make sure we didn't forget anything.

I wasn't even certain I was going with her on this adventure because sometimes, she left me at Alle and Myrtle's house when she went away.

Alle was an overweight (and sometimes overbearing) daschound and Myrtle was some kind of a terrier. Mom used to call them "Lardo and the Terriorist." She never called them that in front of their moms though.

They lived with two nice women and they had a wonderful large yard with trees and squirrels. They also had a huge fig tree and Alle was addicted to figs. No matter what they did, she always found a way to get into the fenced area and eat until her belly touched the ground. Thank goodness it didn't have far to go.

Once, I helped her get into the fenced area. She got in trouble, but I didn't. After that, I didn't help her because I was afraid I'd be in trouble too. I'm glad I wasn't addicted to figs. It was a horrible addiction to try and kick, although, I don't think Alle wanted to kick the habit.

Anyway, mom packed up a tent, sleeping bag, food, wood, all sorts of things. I had no idea why we needed all that stuff, but I still wasn't sure I was going with her.

Finally, she started packing things for me. We took my bed, my special blanket, a large bag of my food, some chicken she had fixed for me, a leash, poop bags and lots of treats. I knew then, I was going.

We drove for a long time, so I slept most of the way. When I woke up, we were pulling onto this little road, lined with trees. She rolled down the windows and we could smell some new fragrances. Mom said she loved the smell of pine trees, so I decided I did too.

The first thing we did was find where we were going to camp and mom put a little sign on it saying it was ours. Good idea; we wouldn't want someone taking our spot.

We went to the boat ramp and she put the boat in the water. It was pretty cool how it sat on top of the water and floated away from the truck. She tied it up on the dock and started loading it with some of the things we had brought with us.

She pulled the truck up the ramp a ways and I ran after her. I didn't want her to leave me there; I didn't know where I was.

We walked back to the boat and she put my bed in it and lifted me onto the bed. I didn't know what to do, so I just sat there. She started the motor and off we went.

At first, I was scared, but then I realized this was how it would feel if I ever got to stick my head out the window of a car. The wind was blowing in my face and the air was clean and soft, just like I had imagined it would be, except, I wasn't in a car.

Pretty soon, she pulled the boat into the shore and I realized we were like at the back door of our camp site, except there was no door. I loved all the freedom of not being confined in a house, or a room. I could explore anywhere I wanted.

I had never seen a lake so I was amazed at all the water. I ran down to the edge and drank. Mom wanted me to drink from the thermos she brought, but why would I when I had all this other water to drink. I could always drink out of the thermos and if the lake ran out of water, that's what I'd do.

Mom was unloading the boat and I suppose I should have helped, but I was busy. There weren't any squirrels around, but there were these little creatures mom called chipmunks and they looked like squirrels, so I chased them.

She pitched a thing called a tent and said that's where we'd sleep. She blew up this big air mattress, put it in the tent and placed a sleeping bag over it.

Before you think I'm really smart and have this big vocabulary, let me explain, mom had to tell me what these things were and what they were for, but once I knew, I never forgot.

I went in the tent and saw she had placed my bed in there also, but I wanted to check out the sleeping bag. She unzipped it and the inside was lined with flannel. I knew where I'd be sleeping. I found out later my bed was used mostly outside the tent, like when I wanted to take an afternoon nap or lie next to the fire at night.

We left the boat down by the lake and once everything was unloaded and in place, mom sat in her chair and I rested on my bed. I was going to take a nap, but every time I closed my eyes, a chipmunk would run through our campsite and I just had to give chase.

Mom fixed dinner for both of us and then we took a walk along the water's edge. I couldn't even see the end of the lake and the more we walked, the more the lake seemed to grow and get larger. Maybe it didn't have an end, I thought.

We were up early and in the boat as the sun came up. Since I'd been in the boat once, I wasn't scared. Mom sat in the back of the boat and I had the whole front end to myself. She put my bed down for me to lie on and covered me with a warm blanket. I was happy because it was cold outside. She put my food dish and water bowl in the boat. She still didn't get it that I had a whole lake to drink from.

The boat slowed down and I looked out from under my blanket to see where we were. I wish I hadn't looked; all I could see was water everywhere. We were nowhere near shore. I wondered if boats ever sank.

Mom was putting things on her fishing pole and let the line out into the water. Kind of seemed like a strange thing to do, but I didn't know how to fish, so I assumed she did.

I had finally settled in and was taking a nap when I heard "fish on". I jumped up, expecting to see something, but all mom was doing was pulling in the line she had just put out.

She grabbed the net which was next to my bed, leaned over the side of the boat and brought in a fish. It came into the boat, flopping around on the floor. I didn't know what to do, so I went over, put my paw on it and licked it.

Mom got a big kick out of that, so I did it every time a fish came in. We'd put them in this ice chest we had with us and mom kept saying we'd have good eating for dinner. Did she really expect me to eat one of those things?

I found out at dinner that night that Kokanee are the best tasting fish in the world; who would have thunk?

Several boats passed us that day, but there weren't many of them. People in the boats would wave and ask how many fish she had, how deep she was trolling and what was she using. Glad they didn't ask me because I had no idea what they were talking about.

Every time I'd come out from under the blanket, she would yell to someone that my name was Andrew and I was her new fishing buddy. I liked the sound of that.

Soon the sun was up and she put up an umbrella to provide some shade for me. I wasn't really that hot, but she said I'd get sunburned. That went right past me.

At one point, she stopped the boat and put some stuff on me. She said it was so I wouldn't burn. I didn't like it one bit until I discovered she put some on herself and we both smelled the same. That was a special sharing moment with my mom.

Finally, she announced we had our limit of fish and we'd have to go to shore and eat some so we could continue fishing later. I still had no idea of what a treat I was in for.

We beached the boat and covered it and headed out for a walk. This was to become my favorite part of the trip because as we headed up a trail that went around the lake, I spotted two deer. Well, I didn't know they were called deer; mom told me later.

As soon as I took out after them they disappeared. They were even faster than I was. Of course, they knew the terrain and I didn't, but I could hear them crashing through the forest, so I followed the sound. I never did catch up with them, but the chase was thrilling. I was exhausted when I came back down the trail.

I have this thing about my mom. She's kind of unpredictable about where she's going, so I have to keep my eye on her.

One time, we were out for our usual morning jaunt and I was chasing rabbits. It was foggy and somehow she managed to get lost in the fog. I looked everywhere for her, but couldn't find her. I didn't know what to do.

Since I knew how to get home from the field we were in, I went on home, without her. I'm coming down the street, taking my sweet time and looking around for her, when all of a sudden, I spotted her in the car; she had gone home to get it to drive around to find me. How lazy can one get?

Anyway, I was a little upset that she had gotten lost and wondered why she left me all alone out there in the fog. She gave me a hug and I gave her a kiss and we forgave each other. But, I never forgot that and always kept my eye on her.

When we went for hikes in the mountains after we had done our fishing, I would do my thing and then stop and look around for her. I think she had learned her lesson because she usually was close by.

I considered getting her some dog tags with her name, address and phone number on them, just in case. Besides, I knew my dog tags made a noise when I was moving and if she had some, maybe they would make noise and it would be easier to find her. She became much better though about staying close.

At lunchtime, we'd cook up two fish, one for me and one for my mom. Let me tell you, that fish meat just melted in my mouth. I could eat Kokanee for every meal.

In the afternoon, we'd relax. Sometimes, we'd go in the tent and take a nap, but I always needed a way out in case I heard some chipmunks or some deer. Usually didn't see many deer in the middle of the day.

Sometimes, I'd rest outside the tent and mom would sit in her chair and read. I didn't know how to read then and I was happy about that because she seemed to be reading boring things, like the rules of golf or something.

One afternoon, I was resting on my bed and mom was reading. There was this chipmunk that kept coming out of a hole near our tent and chattering at me. I hate being chattered at, so I would chase him and he'd always pop down in his hole.

Finally, I just ignored him, until he wandered over near my food dish and stole a piece of my kibble. I was shocked; how dare he?

Now, the gauntlet had been laid down and I was waiting for him to come for more kibble. I'd doze off while I was waiting and that's when he'd come again, grab a piece of kibble and run back to his hole.

I had to put a stop to this, so I took a piece of kibble and dropped it outside his hole and waited. He popped up, grabbed the food and disappeared before I could nab him. I kept repeating this for what seemed like hours.

Mom was laughing at me and suggested I not put the piece so close to his hole. Like what did she know; I was the chipmunk hunter after all.

But, I did come up with a good idea myself. I put the kibble a little farther from the hole, but then I went behind the hole and hid where he couldn't see me.

Up he came and grabbed the food and I jumped between him and the hole and got him. That'll teach him to mess with my food. At least his last meal had been a good one.

Mom was a little upset, but she was amazed at my ingenuity in being able to outsmart the chipmunk. I buried him away from our camp site.

At night, we'd build a big fire and mom would cook over it. I don't know how she did it, but she was good at it. Ever notice that no matter what you cook over a fire, it always tastes better than if you fixed the same thing at home? Try it sometime.

We'd go for a long walk before bedtime, usually along the water's edge. It was kind of scary walking through the tall trees as the sun was setting. You never knew what you might run into when it got dark.

My favorite fishing trip of all time was when mom turned fifty. In dog years, I guess that meant she was really old. We rented a houseboat and were gone for days.

It was neat. We got to sleep in actual beds and not in a tent on the ground; it was high class.

Different friends of hers would drop in and spend a couple of days with us and then leave and new ones would come in. Every morning, we'd take people out in the boat and catch Kokanee.

At night, someone would be the designated driver, which meant she didn't get to drink any champagne and we'd do these sunset dinner trips around the lake.

The boat had a grill on it and we'd cook up the fish we'd caught and pig out. The people ate salads and stuff, but I only wanted the fish.

We'd come back to shore, tie the houseboat up and build a big fire on the beach. The people would tell stories, laugh and try to sing. The Mormon Tabernacle Choir they were not, but it was fun anyway.

A couple of them had too much to drink and one of them fell in the lake, or maybe she was pushed, I don't know. She went to bed before any of the rest of us.

I think every dog should have a chance to be on a houseboat at least once in their lives; what an experience. Anyone who came was not allowed to bring any children or husbands with them, but they could bring their dogs.

Some of the dogs didn't know how to camp or fish for that matter. I was the only dog who got to go out fishing in the boat. There wouldn't have been room for them anyway.

Rita - Fishing/Camping

WHEN I FIRST HEARD WE were going fishing, I was somewhat perturbed. It meant I had to get up earlier in the morning than usual. This is a girl who likes to sleep in. I already was unhappy about the early mornings we kept, but to get up way before dawn and to leave home before the sun came up, was out of the question.

I went along because I was afraid I'd miss out on something if I didn't go. I was assured it was just for one day and we'd be back in time to go rabbit hunting in the afternoon.

Changing my routine was not something I liked to do and I thought I had trained my human to understand that. If I'd have come up with that idea, it would have been okay, but I had no say in it.

We arrived at the lake and I jumped out immediately. I had to do my stuff. While I was doing it, my human started backing the boat towards the water. I was afraid she'd leave me and I didn't know where we were.

I hate water. I will walk two blocks out of my way so I don't get hit by the sprinklers in someone's yard, but when my human walked into the water to shove the boat off the trailer, I followed her.

You won't believe what she did next; she took out her camera and took a picture of me in the water. There went my image. I know she sent it to a lot of people who know how I hate water.

The problem for me arose when she thought I should get in the boat. It was bobbing up and down in the water at the end of the dock and it didn't look too stable to me.

She'd put me in the boat and then when she'd try to get in, I'd jump out. Finally, she held me while she climbed in and pushed us away from the dock. I knew then it was too late to jump out; I'd really be in some water.

As I am prone to do when a new situation arises which seems to be out of my control, I look things over and then take charge. I assumed all boats had a captain, so I went to the bow of the ship and took over, like I knew where we were going.

Quickly, I sat down on my bed because my human gunned it and we were moving quickly across the water. I knew instinctively that I did not want to fall out.

By the time we reached our fishing spot, I was pretty comfortable being in my boat. Of course, we slowed down so she could troll.

I settled in on my bed and was covered by my blanket. I tried to sleep, but felt I needed to keep an eye on things, just in case my human didn't know what she was doing. We had been together long enough for me to realize that she did not have the answer for everything.

I had just dozed off when the boat stopped moving, so I stuck my head out to see what was happening. My human was standing up in the boat and turning a handle on the end of a long pole.

Soon I saw a fish jump out of the water and I became interested. I'm not sure what happened, but I never saw the fish again and my human was swearing. I don't think I missed anything.

Next thing I knew, she was bending over the boat with a net in her hand and trapped a fish in it. I'd never been close to a real live fish before, so I went over and stuck my head in the net. The fish was flopping all around and my human was pushing me away because she was trying to get the hook out of its mouth.

We plopped that baby into the ice chest and she said we would eat him later. I wasn't too sure about eating something that flops around, but I'm pretty much known as a garbage hound that will eat anything, so I figured I'd give it a try.

Let me tell you, until you eat a fresh Kokanee, you haven't eaten at all. My human cooked up three of them and I ate almost all of two of them—delicious.

I wondered why we didn't just buy some at the store and not waste all that time traveling and being out on the water, but my human says they are a protected game fish and you can't buy them anywhere.

Humans have so many things they protect, and yet, some of the things they should protect, they don't. I think humans either protect something or abuse it; thank goodness I'm not a human.

After the fishing, we went for a long hike. I wanted to go along the entire trail, but apparently, it never ends, so we turned back after a while.

It was great because I was able to chase chipmunks all along the way. They are a lot like squirrels except they have funny stripes on them. They also aren't as much fun as squirrels because they won't run very far. Chipmunks either climb a tree or disappear into their holes, but the chase was fun.

Then, I saw something I'd never seen before. My human said it was a deer, which, of course, meant nothing to me. All I knew was that it was on four legs and ran like crazy.

I took off after one, but it disappeared as quickly as it came into view. I could hear it thrashing through the trees and I followed the noise, but I never saw it again.

One thing I learned early on in my life is you don't chase anything that can fly; it's an exercise in futility. I mean, how can a dog expect to catch anything whose feet leave the ground?

Unlike humans who often chase after something they'll never get, dogs only go for the things they have a chance at. Oh, I know, there are some dogs who try to chase birds, ducks and geese, but really, they look ridiculous when they try.

By now, I'm tired and ready to go home. After all, I have friends who will be waiting to go rabbit hunting with me. But, my human says we are going to spend the night and fish again in the morning.

Being too tired to argue with her, I lay down on my bed and watched as she set up our camp, as she called it. Sure looked like a lot of work to me.

When she went to put up the tent (this is the camping part of the trip) she became agitated. Supposedly, a tent is like a little room you erect, throw all your things in it and then sleep in it.

My human began swearing again because there are some poles you use to push the tent up into the air so there's room to walk into the tent. She must have forgotten them. I didn't know how to help her because I didn't know how to camp in the first place.

We built a fire after she spent hours trying to make the tent work without poles. After dinner, she pumped up an air mattress and put it on top of the tent which was lying on the ground. Then she put a sleeping bag over it. I knew I was not going to be happy with these arrangements.

A nice long walk along the lake's edge seemed to calm my human's nerves, but mine were just starting to go wild. It was getting dark, I wasn't home, and I didn't see any bed for me to sleep in.

What a horrible night that first night was. Deer kept tromping through our campsite and my human grabbed me each time they did. She didn't want me chasing them in the dark. I don't think I would have gotten lost.

There was a bright moon out, so it wasn't completely dark, but the air was cold and we both had to snuggle up close in the sleeping bag. At least it had flannel sheets. She slept in her clothes. I'd never known her to do that.

Then, there were these weird sounds all night long. I didn't know what they were and they scared me. My human said they were coyotes. I wanted no part of them.

After all we'd been through, we caught more fish the next day and I knew we'd have good eating later. My human packed up all our stuff and we headed home. I got there in time for my afternoon rabbit hunt. Koki and Osito could not believe what I went through and said they hoped they wouldn't ever have to go camping with us.

I will say this, the next time we went camping, my human remembered everything. It was so much more restful in a tent where we could hide from cold air, deer and coyotes, but I still wanted to get out and chase them in the dark. I thought I'd have a better chance if they couldn't see me. Of course, I'd have to lose the collar; they would be able to hear my dog tags clanging from a mile away.

On one of our trips, my human took me to this mountain top where she said she would build a nine-hole golf course if she ever won the lottery. She pointed out where each hole would go and how she would preserve the natural beauty of the land on each hole.

I don't know much about golf, but if she preserved the land, her golf course would be the most difficult one to play because there would be a tree or a hazard every step of the way.

Humans like to dream, so I let her have her dream. After all, what were the chances of her winning the lottery? As far as I knew, she never even bought a lottery ticket.

Dogs have dreams also, but our dreams are of things that are actually attainable, like catching a big rabbit or two squirrels at one time. Ever watch us sleep? Our legs look like we're running, our bodies twitch and shake and we make funny noises through it all.

My favorite camping trip was when we went to our favorite lake (the one where Andrew, my human and me will end up at). Two of my human's sisters and their husbands showed up. I think one other was not invited. And, the woman who had taken care of my human's mother before she died went with us. She was a sort of a sister to my human.

We had a blast! We had plenty of food and there was more than enough for the dogs. Oh, yes, the dogs. One sister brought her two dogs, but they were not very well behaved, or maybe they just didn't like me, but I find that hard to believe.

They were chained up most of the time because they got out of hand. One time, they got loose and started after me. I always laugh when a dog chases me because it is such a hopeless cause for them.

I went up the trail and towards the parking lot; they followed. Behind them was my human's sister and her husband, but no one else came. My human knows that whichever way I run, just turn around and go the opposite way.

So, here are these two dogs and two humans thinking they are chasing me, but I had already cut down the boat ramp, came along the shore and was back in camp before they even knew they had lost me.

My human knew I'd come up behind them, so she and the others waited for me. By the time the other dogs came back, they were exhausted and I was well rested.

I had my first taste of champagne on that trip. Oh, my human didn't give me any, but they were drinking the stuff to celebrate something and when they'd had too much, it was easy to meander over near a glass and help myself. Boy, and I thought beer tasted good. I could drink champagne every day. Everyone slept well that night.

We stayed several days. The fishing was great and it was fun to watch a human family in action. Certainly not like any family I've been around.

The humans were all related, but they all did things separately. They all slept in separate tents, went fishing in separate boats and even cooked separate things for dinner.

When I had my pups, we all did everything together whether we wanted to or not. But, we all got to know each other well and when it was time to go our separate ways, we did it. No one stuck around to see if there was anything they might do together as a family.

We parted on good terms and no one ever bitched about each other or complained about each other. If humans want to continue trying to keep their families together, they need to learn how not to judge one another or have unreasonable expectations of each other.

I love to go camping and fishing with my human because she pretty much has let me run things. She's just there to get the boat in and out of the water and catch fresh fish for me to eat.

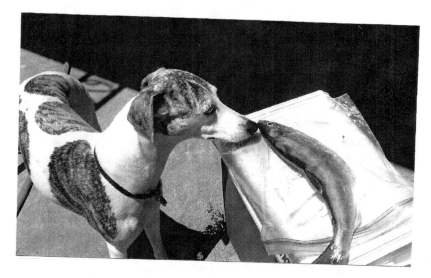

Rita checking out dinner

Andrew — Entitlements

ENTITLEMENTS—A WORD USED A LOT in the world of humans. I think it means something that humans think is owed to them whether they deserve them or not.

Dogs are deserving of many things also. Whether we are entitled to them is another question. Some things we want or need must be earned. Just because we exist is not a good reason for having things.

Because of our nature and our ability to give unconditional love, I think we are entitled to a good home where we are safe, cared for and loved. All living creatures deserve that.

Basic needs for all seem to be food, clothing, shelter and clean water. I can forgo the clothing stuff. I find sweaters and other articles designed to keep me warm, limit my ability to run, and if I can run, I can keep warm.

Whippets don't have much body fat and I certainly don't have much fur, but I know how to keep warm anyway without human clothing.

Since humans think it is cute to dress their dogs in costumes appropriate for a given season, or because they look adorable in some kinds of clothing, is no reason for me to want any part of it, though I have to admit, I did look good in a muscle shirt my mom bought me. I wore it twice and then figured how to get it off.

There always seems to be enough food for me and I hope there's enough for my mom too. As long as she doesn't forget to give me the chicken I've become addicted to, we'll be fine.

When my heart started to give out, my vet asked what I ate. Mom told her and she commented that perhaps the chicken wasn't the best thing for me to eat.

Mom thought about that for a while and then decided I should be able to eat what I wanted during the last part of my life. She said if she had a bad heart, no one would tell her what she could and couldn't eat. She's pretty sensible about those things.

Every year when we went to the vet, she'd report that my heart murmur was another point higher. When I reached level five, my mom asked what the highest level was for a dog to live. The vet said level six was the highest. Mom and I both knew it was only a matter of time.

I wasn't supposed to be out chasing rabbits and running around so much, but it was something I loved doing. Mom would limit my running at times, and I didn't get to chase anything on hot summer afternoons.

But, we'd go out early in the morning when it was cool. Besides, I kind of knew I wasn't able to do the things I had been able to do when I was younger.

I used to chase a rabbit as far as I could until he escaped through a fence or something. I monitored myself and paced myself pretty well. I'd only run for a while and then walk back to mom, until another rabbit happened by, but I really couldn't go all out like I had in the past.

The same kind of thing was happening to my mom also. She often said she couldn't do the same things she had done twenty years ago. We both got tired easier than we had and so we took afternoon naps together; it was something we were entitled to because we had earned the right to do that.

Of course, I believe dogs are entitled to have flannel sheets on the bed. Not all dogs get to sleep under the covers like I did, but if they did, they were entitled to flannel sheets.

Dogs are entitled to be treated like members of the families they live with. They are, after all, true members of those families. We protect our people, love them and would do anything we could for them. We are entitled to share in their activities and pleasures.

We are there when they are sad, angry, happy or whatever. We are entitled to not be shut out of their lives just because we are dogs. My mom would take me any place she could and if we had to stay in a motel or a friend's house, I had to be included.

One time we were on a long trip up to Oregon and needed to stay in a hotel our first night out. She checked before we left home to see which hotels I was welcomed at. We checked into a hotel in Ashland. What a place! They gave us a room with a door leading to the outside next to a fenced-in area put there just for the dogs to use. It was a nice touch.

That night when we went to bed, mom pulled down the covers and there was a mint on one of the pillows, but there were two dog biscuits on the other pillow. We stayed at the same place every time we made the trip.

Sometimes you find little entitlements you didn't even know existed. When we stayed at grandma and grandpa's house, they set up one of their couches just for me.

Grandpa would get himself a snack around nine in the evening. I always went to bed long before that, but when I'd hear the refrigerator door open. I'd drag my tired butt out from under the covers and take my little blood-shot eyes into the kitchen.

This was another unexpected entitlement for me because Grandpa always said we were both entitled to a treat at the end of the day if we had been good, and we both always were.

It was special with him because I got to help choose our snack. He'd grab two or three things out and let me smell them. I'd gently lick the one I wanted. Usually, I chose some cheese; he was pleased with my choices. He'd get some crackers out of the cupboard and I'd sit by his chair and we'd dine together.

After he died, mom and I went to visit grandma. It wasn't the same without him, but we all knew he'd want us to carry on. Grandma insisted we all have cheese and crackers every night. At one point, she made mom and me get into grandpa's chair. She said no one had sat there since he left and we had to get over it.

If my mom was sad about something, she would cry. I never knew quite what to do about it, so I would wash the tears from her face and sit quietly next to her.

Dogs don't quite experience sadness the way humans do. It's not that things don't upset us, but we don't belabor those moments and move on to something more pleasant.

We also don't experience pain the same way humans do. Sure, I hurt a lot when I got hit by that truck, but I think my mom was hurting more than me. That bothered me a whole lot more than my own pain. Dogs seem to be able to feel others pains easier than humans can.

Plus, if there is something a dog really wants to do, we can forget all about the pain and just do it.

I had kind of sprained one of my legs one time and was hobbling around, but when I saw a rabbit running across the field, I forgot all about the pain and took off after him.

It's too bad humans cannot give unconditional love because I think dogs should be entitled to that wonderful gift, but, humans have egos that we don't have, so it is impossible for them to love that way. At least dogs are entitled to all the love a human can possibly give.

Humans should realize they are entitled to unconditional love from a dog. Many of them do not recognize unconditional love, don't understand it, and thus, they are incapable of totally accepting the gift we offer them and that's too bad, because they miss out on so much.

~One thing I feel every living creature should be entitled to is the right to die with dignity and without suffering too much.

For many, when their time is up, they pass on quickly, always with dignity and without suffering. My spirits had informed me that it was time for me to move on to my next adventure. This was shortly after the vet said my heart murmur had reached level six.

I fought with my spirit because I didn't want to leave my human; I knew she would be so sad and lost without me. She had already lost so many in her life.

I struggled to keep myself alive and the vet was surprised each time I went back in. At one point she said there must be a level seven. My murmur was so bad, you didn't even need a stethoscope to hear it. The last time I was there, the vet would not give me my shots because she said it would compromise my immune system.

So, guess what happened? The sheriff sent a letter saying I would be taken into custody if mom did not get me vaccinated. I didn't want to go to jail; I knew I would die there without mom.

The vet took care of it and told the sheriff about my condition. At the same time I was failing, grandma was failing also. When we went to visit her, I knew she wasn't going to be around much longer.

During the last visit, she and I looked at each other for a long time; we both knew it was our last visit, but grandma conveyed to me it was time for her to move on and be with grandpa.

She also told me she knew I wasn't well and she and grandpa would be happy to see me soon. I wish she had told mom that she would be there for me.

About a month after grandma died, my spirits told me my time was up. I still didn't want to leave my mom, but somehow, they made her spirits realize I had to go.

She held me when they gave me the shot. Neither of us could look at each other. She was brave and did the right thing. I moved on with dignity and peacefully. I think at the end she showed she could love me unconditionally.

Every day she still talks to me and every day, I am still there in her heart, giving her my unconditional love. She'll never get over me, but my job here was completed.

My spirits and I knew she needed another dog in her life and I wasn't sure Rita was the right one, but I was assured her task on earth was different from mine and mom needed a dog to take her in new directions.

Mom was entitled to be loved again.

I just wish Rita weren't so bossy, but maybe that's what mom needed—a challenge.

Andrew and Grandpa enjoying a snack

Rita — Entitlements

HUMANS ARE SO SELFISH; THEY think they are entitled to everything.

They think they are entitled to a good job where they don't have to do much, but get paid a lot of money. They think someone else should pay for their health insurance and health care for that matter.

Humans think they are entitled to a new car every year, the biggest television set available, all the latest electronic gadgets, good schools and good teachers, all without having to pay too much of any of it.

When something goes wrong in their lives, or they suffer some kind of a setback, they moan, "Why me?" What makes them think they should be immune to life's little tosses and turns? What makes them think they are better than anyone else?

And, things do go wrong in life—everyone's life. Recently, the human economy took a big turn for the worse—disastrous almost, but it hit everyone and some people just couldn't adjust or cope with it.

People started losing their houses—houses they had bought because they thought they were entitled to something they couldn't afford. The old American dream of owning a home had gotten out of hand. Owning a home and owning a home you can afford, are two different things.

Of course, there were those humans who believed they were entitled to take other people's money and do whatever they wanted to with it. Why would they want to do it? Greed! Why would people trust someone else with all their money? Greed!

It's hard to imagine that people could be so gullible that they think they are entitled to more than they deserve. What happened to the days when folks took care of themselves, didn't rack up huge amounts of debt and took responsibility for their own actions?

Oh, well, those days have been long gone; no use crying over spilt milk now.

Let me tell you about an incident my human and I saw on television one night. I still howl about it every time I think of it.

We live in California and the economy here really got out of hand. Everyone, including the government, was living and spending way beyond what they could afford, and they all thought they were entitled to do that.

Well, the state announced that its employees would have to take two furlough Fridays off each month to help get the budget back in balance. This was being done in hopes of not having to lay off a lot of state workers.

Oh, my goodness, the hue and cry of the workers was unbelievable. Never mind they still had a job while workers in many other areas had no job; they were pissed about giving up two days of pay a month. Some of those people could have taken more days off and no one would have noticed.

Anyway, the evening news interviewed a married couple who both worked for the state. Here they were a man and a woman crying over the furlough. They had no idea how they were going to make ends meet. Both of them were sitting on a couch. They were so large there would not have been room for one more person to sit. Cutting back on food seemed like a good idea to me for a cost cutting measure. Might have helped any health issues they had too.

They were concerned about perhaps having to sell one of their cars; they didn't say how many they had, but they might have to sell one.

My human did the math. They were each losing $400 a day twice a week. That meant each one of them would only be bringing home $7200 a month instead of $8000, for a combined total of $14,400 and not $16,000 they felt they were entitled to.

I could just hear the hearts of workers making minimum wage and retirees on social security breaking for them. Thank goodness the homeless and unemployed probably didn't have a television set to watch this fiasco or they would have been weeping also.

These people felt they were entitled to something better than having to take furlough days. How could this happen to them?

But, they stole my heart when they said that because of the furlough days, they were not able to send anything to their son at Christmas time while he was serving in Iraq. It made me want to barf.

Where do humans get off thinking things should be given to them just because they are humans?

Humans over-indulge in almost every aspect of their lives and feel they are entitled to do this. They overeat, overspend, over drink, and if any of this behavior causes any health problems, they are entitled to have someone else foot the bill for them.

They overindulge with the "toys" they think they are entitled to like televisions, computers, games, cars, houses, gadgets, maids, gardeners; oh the list goes on and on.

Ever wonder how many people make a living just by providing services to overindulgent people? Unfortunately, they do all the work, but do not make all the money.

Humans always think they are worth more than they get paid and there is usually someone there to see that they get paid more than they are worth.

Excuse me, but is there really any one person out there who is worth ten million dollars a year, or more? Heads of companies, sports stars, movie stars and others seem to think they are worth more than ten mil a year and they get it.

And what do they do with all that wealth and power? They cheat on their spouses, abuse their children and other family members, commit crimes and bribe others to look away.

Why is it the ones who make the most money get the most perks? You make a lot of money, you get free health insurance, a company car or maybe a plane. You're a star so when you go out to dinner, you get comped for it. Here, wear our clothes; it won't cost you a thing.

All the while, the average person has to pay for everything. Where's the equity in life? There is none because some people really believe they are entitled to more than the average person.

Humans need to take a look at what is really important in this life and get back to some basic entitlements. Food, shelter, clothing, water—are all essential things for a good life.

An entitlement should be earned, not taken for granted. An example is social security; people pay into that system all their lives. They are entitled to get back what they put in when they are no longer working.

If they have saved their money faithfully over the years, they are entitled to get that back when they need it.

Humans are entitled to not be screwed over by unscrupulous beings that provide services and products to them.

But, I'm getting away from the important things—my entitlements.

I'm entitled to be fed, housed and cared for in a way that's becoming for me. This means be sure to stock up on those $5 chickens on Fridays at Safeway because I'm entitled to have chicken scattered over my dog food daily.

This means ordering enough beef jerky for me and my friends. Fortunately, my human has a nice jerky gig going for us. Her dad started a jerky factory in Oregon.

Now, it is owned by some other people and they make a jerky designed for dogs. Of course, people can eat it too and it contains less salt than normal jerky. My human and I both like it.

This stuff is called Bit O Luv and you can order it in two pound bags. She calls the manager there and orders bunches of bags. I probably shouldn't let this out, but dogs are entitled to good treats. Go to www.oberto.com. Tell John Rita sent you.

ENTITLEMENT MEANS HAVING FLOOR VENTS in the house so I can lay next to them for warmth in the winter and cool air in the summer. It means flannel sheets on the bed until it is too hot for them to be comfortable.

It means letting me sleep in until the sun comes up and then taking me out to chase squirrels and rabbits. Three times a day is good for chasing critters, and as I age, twice a day will probably do.

It means taking me to visit humans who also have dogs and letting me steal any food they left in their dish and eating any treats left on the floor. And, if I find a toy I really like, I can steal it on my way out the door.

I am entitled to not have to wear cute sweaters, costumes or other articles of human clothing. If God had wanted me in a sweater, I would have been born with one. I am entitled to not have to do tricks for treats or any other reason. The fact that I am here, am beautiful and in charge, should be enough.

If I am ever a guest in someone's home because my human decided to go somewhere without me on the assumption she was entitled to get away, then I am entitled to be treated like royalty. I need my own couch and I'll bring my own blanket.

When the humans retire for the evening, I'm entitled to snoop through the house to see if there's anything I want, like potato chips, Cheeze-Its, or any other snack. I'm entitled to stash them behind my couch in case I need them later, or if my human doesn't return when I think she should.

Everyone knows I enjoy ice cubes and they think it is so cute how I eat them. What is so cute about a dog crunching quickly and with her mouth open on cold ice cubes?

I do think, however, that I am entitled to ice cubes with a little more flavor than the ones which come out of a freezer. Margaritas, vodka tonics and other such flavors come to mind.

I think that if my human is entitled to have a beer, then I should be entitled to share it with her.

Riding shotgun in anyone's car is an entitlement I deserve. I should not be stuck in a back seat with other dogs. Besides, I know where we're going and I know how to lean into the curve to help stabilize the vehicle.

I'm entitled to pick my own friends which is hard because there just aren't many dogs out there who are worthy of my friendship and the ones who are have the same attitude problems I have. They do make good friends because we can work out systems without having to tell our humans about them.

If I'm required to be a friend because a dog belongs to a friend of my human, I'm entitled to ignore that dog forever, if I choose to do so.

In other words, if humans are allowed to have all the entitlements they think they deserve, then I don't want anyone to argue with me over my entitlements.

Andrew — Happiness

HAPPINESS IS A BEAUTIFUL WORD and a wonderful feeling. For some, it takes a lot to make them happy, but it doesn't take much for me because I'm happy most of the time.

You can tell when a dog is happy because he'll wag his tail, roll in the grass, give kisses even when they aren't wanted, greet you at the door when you come home and snore peacefully under the covers as he snuggles close.

Hard to tell sometimes when humans are happy; they don't do the same things dogs do—maybe they should try it.

Perhaps dogs are happy most of the time because of their ability to love unconditionally. We have no expectations and try to make no judgments of others.

We are like humans in that those we judge most harshly are our fellow dogs. I would never criticize a human for being lazy or stupid, but I sure can let another dog know when he's not acting in an appropriate manner.

Humans tend to look to others for their happiness. They count on friends, relatives, even strangers to do something to make them happy. They really don't get it that happiness comes from within.

They get caught up in the complexity and business of their lives; they don't take time to smell the roses or any other flower for that matter.

I have a simple life. I make no specific plans, schedules or have an agenda that I and everyone around me must follow. I delight in common things.

Like all creatures, I have needs and I do rely on my mom to help me meet those needs, but I don't depend on her for my own happiness.

I can take pleasure in eating everyday and an occasional treat will bring more happiness than one could expect. I love to run and chase things and when I get to do that, happiness oozes through my veins.

When I'm tired, I take a nap and rest up for the joys that await me when I awake. Humans don't take the time to refresh themselves and keep going even when they are tired. It's hard to be happy when you are tired, rushing around and not getting things done.

I love to go for rides even if I'm not going any place in particular. Humans always want to be going somewhere.

Sometimes, just getting out in a beautiful setting and enjoying nature can make me happy. I love to see trees (and not just so I can mark them), but I love the smell of trees.

Running in the sand at the beach thrills me. You don't see too many humans running on the beach and having a great time.

I marvel at all my surroundings and am happy with all I see, sense, smell and experience.

Well, almost all my surroundings. There was one time I wasn't too thrilled with what I encountered. My mom used to take me to this area outside of town. It was along a levee with a creek below it. There were lots of trees, bushes and stuff to run through.

There were also a lot of critters out there to chase. One day, I think it was in January because it was kind of cold outside, we went to the levee. Mom was bundled up and walking fast to keep warm.

I was running and searching for something to chase. I heard a noise in one of the bushes and went to explore. I saw this funny looking creature and moved closer to see what it was. As I drew near, I noticed it had some babies with it. They were very small and black in color.

Since I never mess with anyone's babies, I stopped and just looked. Mothers don't like to have strangers around their young children and I knew that, but I was curious about them. I wasn't going to chase them or hurt them. You know, it was kind of one of those "Aw" moments.

Well, mama moved between me and the babies, turned her back to me and the next thing I knew, she sprayed me with some really stinky stuff. It didn't hurt, but phew, did it stink.

I left immediately and continued on my way. I found my mom and ran to tell her what I'd seen, but as soon as I got near her, she knew exactly what I'd seen—it was a skunk!

We had to ride home with all the windows down in the car and the heater on full blast. We nearly froze to death.

Needless to say, I had to have a bath. Usually, I don't care for a bath, but I knew this one was necessary to get the smell off me. I thought I was going to throw up.

Mom was laughing and holding her nose the entire time. I didn't think it was funny. Besides, it is no fun to come out of a warm bath into the cold winter air.

She had been told that washing a dog in tomato juice would get rid of the skunk smell, so she went to the store to get the juice. She used way too much and it was kind of sticky. Once she washed it off, it wasn't too bad, but it didn't all wash off.

Now I know dogs are not supposed to be able to see colors, but I knew I was not the same color I had been before she washed me. The white parts of my fur looked pink to me. Mom confirmed that I did look a little pink.

One of her friends suggested she wash me again in lemon juice, so we tried that. It did smell better than the skunk did, but it did nothing for the pink tint I was wearing.

For days, I would not go outside in the daylight. I couldn't take the chance one of my friends would see me. Fortunately in January, there are fewer hours of daylight than darkness. We'd go out in the mornings before sunrise and I wouldn't go out again until after dark.

For what seemed like years after that incident, every time I'd get wet, you could smell the skunk again. That was probably the only time I wasn't very happy, but I got over it.

Humans don't get over being unhappy easily. They seem to dwell on their unhappiness, blame someone else for it and wallow around trying to find something that will make them happy.

All you have to do is look inside and see the person you are. What else do you need to be happy? You don't need some big event or occasion to be happy; be happy with little things and bigger ones will come flowing into your life.

My mom says she is happy every day that she wakes up. I don't totally understand that—why wouldn't she wake up? We both wake up every morning and that makes both of us happy.

Starting out our day being happy brings more happiness to each of us. I guess that's because we both know we'll be together and do things we both enjoy.

Mom goes golfing sometimes after we've been out for our morning run (she walks, I run). She says it makes her happy to golf, but then she comes home and complains about how she played golf. What happened to being happy about playing a game she loves?

Funny how humans continue to do things that don't make them happy. If mom is unhappy about how she played golf, why does she go back out and do it again? I never went back out to find a skunk.

With dogs, things either make you happy or they don't, and when they don't, you stay away from doing the same things over and over again.

With humans, things can make you happy at times and unhappy at other times; they are too complicated that way. When mom plays golf well, she is like floating on a cloud. Someday she will have to learn that just playing golf is a happy thing, no matter how you play.

I'm glad I don't have a job, other than taking care of my mom, because when humans have a job, they always fluctuate between being happy and unhappy.

Sometimes mom would come home from work and be unhappy. She'd be swearing about one thing or another, take a shower, maybe have a cold beer and continue complaining. She'd stop and look at me. I'd give her a big kiss, run to the car and we'd go out and do something happy, like chase rabbits. She loved to watch me run and I'd do silly things like run around trees, stop and go back the other way; it made her laugh and she'd be happy again; I was doing my job.

But, she'd get up in the morning and go back out to work, hoping that day wouldn't be as bad as the previous one.

When she retired, mom was very happy. Her life became more uncomplicated, like mine. We had more time for each other and I was able to take better care of her. Oh, she still golfed, but she didn't come home unhappy any more.

We had more time to fish, camp and hike; we both loved doing that.

When I wasn't able to run and chase rabbits like I used to, we'd go for long walks downtown and she'd take me past all the restaurants and bakeries where I'd scrounge around for treats. Once I found part of a hamburger, a piece of pizza and part of a loaf of bread.

I usually didn't eat the stuff I found because I kind of thought if someone had thrown it away, they probably weren't any good, so I'd take them somewhere and bury them. I had stuff buried all around town. Sometimes, I go back and check to see if they were still there; they usually were, but they were soggy and all dirty.

As I got older, most of my old friends had died or moved away. I learned that it didn't make me unhappy not to see them anymore. I just remembered how happy I was that they had been in my life.

We found some new friends. Koki and Osito were Shiba Inus that belong with a guy named David and we started walking with them. It was nice to be around them because they were always happy and fun to be with.

Osito was a real character. She was even more of a garbage hound than I was and she'd find some of the strangest things to eat. David was always on her case about what she was eating, but it sure made her happy to find something she knew she shouldn't eat.

I have been blessed with a happy life, a good mom, wonderful friends and neighbors and I wouldn't trade my life for anyone else's. I hope my mom feels the same way.

Rita - Happiness

HAPPINESS? WHAT THE HELL DOES that mean? You know there's an old saying—"if your dog ain't happy, ain't nobody happy."

Okay, so maybe you didn't hear it the same way I did, but let's face it, if you have an unhappy dog, she can make your life miserable and you know it.

Trust me; it's a lot easier to have a happy dog than to have a happy human. Humans can make themselves unhappy at any given point in time; they are good at it. Humans expect too much, demand too much and blame each other for their unhappiness.

A human cannot blame a dog for their unhappiness. One of the main reason humans are happy as often as they are is because they have a dog.

You've heard the adages about the more I'm around people, the more I like my dog, or the one about put your wife and your dog in the trunk of a car and see which one is happy to see you when you open the trunk.

Dogs know how to treat humans better than humans treat each other. Who complains about how you look or what you're wearing—your spouse or your dog?

Who cares whether or not you drink the orange juice right from the container or from a glass? Who cares whether you pick up your stuff or not?

Actually, dogs like it when you don't pick things up because it gives them more toys to play with. And, it doesn't matter to a dog whether or not you put the seat down on the toilet, just don't close the entire thing off so we can't get a drink of water.

Maybe it is easier for dogs to be happy because they have an easier life. We don't have the same pressures humans have, but if you stop and think about it, it's really the humans who put the pressures on themselves.

However, being a dog and having to take care of a human is not an easy task. While humans are fairly easy to train, it still takes a lot of time and patience to get them to do what you want them to do. If only they'd learn that doing it our way makes for a happier life.

I admit, I was not particularly happy about being kidnapped from my first home. In fact, it may have been the one time I was truly unhappy, but did I cry and moan and belittle the humans who were responsible?

Okay, maybe I did some of that, but I got over it. Just because some little thing went wrong, I didn't have to go see a therapist or take some kind of drugs to get my life back together. Dogs are much more resilient than humans in that way.

Every time there was a setback in training my new human, I was able to recover and get her back eating out of my paw. Even the thing with the dog training collar worked to my advantage.

When David told her I was running amok after she had fallen and wasn't able to be in charge of things, I managed to turn that unpleasantness around.

The only thing that irked me was when she'd turn that damn collar on, it would beep five times and she'd always say, "Oh, Rita, it's for you."

Humans can be so stupid about these things. Of course, I knew it was for me and I knew right off the bat that she thought zapping me would get me to do things her way. You notice she only had to zap me twice.

Sometimes, she'd put the collar on me and forget to turn it on. Do you think I ever let her know that I knew it wasn't on? Hell, no; I let her think she had me where she wanted me. One time she forgot to bring the zapper part with her, so it didn't matter whether it was turned on or not.

I turned that whole thing around by keeping my eye on her. I'd go and do my thing like I always do and when I'd think she was lost or not keeping close to me, I'd go back and stare at her, like where have you been. It works every time. Now, she lends that collar to other humans who think their dogs are running amok.

I got a big laugh out of one of her friends who put the collar on her dog. No matter how many times she zapped that dog, it would stop, bark at her and then continue on its way. We have the collar back. I would have done that, too, but I didn't want my human to think she had any control whatsoever.

I've heard all the stories about Andrew so I know he was a big mama's boy and thought his world revolved around his human. He could be happy no matter what happened.

I'm different; I'm not a mama's girl. It's more like I'm her precious little princess and I can do what I want, that is if you want us both to be happy.

Don't get me wrong; I don't abuse the relationship. My human takes good care of me and loves me. She even thinks some of my antics are cute, but I'm not going to change who I am just for her.

I would never ask her to change for me, but she's smart; she knows if she doesn't change and do things my way, she won't be happy.

Why do things have to be my way? I'll tell you why. I'm easy-going, don't expect much from anyone and I don't ask for much in return. Humans want and expect too much from each other and from their dogs. If they just slow down, go with the flow and relax, life will be a dream.

I don't swear too much, I forget and forgive quickly so I move on to other things and my way produces results. After all, don't we both get some wonderful exercise by going rabbit hunting? Don't we both enjoy visiting with friends and neighbors and don't they all get a kick out my stealing toys and other dog's food?

If they didn't enjoy themselves when I'm around, why would everyone give me treats when I come to visit?

Perhaps if I were a human, people wouldn't put up with me, but I'm a dog and am allowed certain freedoms and actions humans can't enjoy.

I know my place and my role in my human's life; I take as good care of her as she will allow. She's the one with limitations and problems; I have none.

I was sad when Micki died, but I knew it was time for her to move on to a new adventure. I was happy I got to know her. However, when her replacement, Lola, moved in, I was not too happy.

First off, Lola is a Boston Terrier, which can also be spelled Terrorist. She's young, has no idea how to train her humans and has way too much nervous energy.

I will work with Lola and show her the ropes. She's not stupid, so I can teach her how to channel her energy into good things. Her human needs to go to obedience school with her so she can learn how to be trained.

Lola should make for a good hunting partner. She's fast and probably has never had the chance to chase squirrels and rabbits; she'll love it. I've already shown her how to roll in the grass and chill out a little. She even picked up on how good grass is to eat.

Her human said she likes ice cubes, so once the margaritas start flowing, we should get along just fine. She'll get her human trained and I'll get Lola trained to do things my way.

So, what is happiness? You really can't define it and no explanation of happiness in a dictionary does it justice.

Happiness is that feeling you get when your world is in place and you know how to deal with it. Happiness comes from within you and can be shared with anyone. There is nothing you can do that will make someone else happy unless they want it to.

Being happy means you are pleased with yourself and where you are going, and if the road gets a little rough, you go around the problem and continue on.

At any given point in time, you can say you are happy because you want to be.

When I'm not happy about something, I will do whatever it takes to change my unhappiness. Remember the dog beds and having all my friends around me staring at my human to let her know I'm unhappy. The situation can always be handled quickly and I can return to being happy.

If my human is unhappy, it's up to her to do something about it, but I'm always there with a kiss or to clean her hands. I can even share a bowl of ice cream or a sip or two of beer if it makes her happy.

Rita's Post Script

I INSISTED ON BEING ALLOWED one more chapter than Andrew received because I still have a few things to say and we didn't have a chapter that my thoughts fit into.

As I'm sure you have gathered, I do have many opinions about most topics and there are a couple I really need to share with everyone.

It appears nearly everyone is facing some kind of budget or economic crisis and our cities, states and government agencies have been hit very hard.

Of course, if they had managed all their money (which they receive from its citizens) this would not be such a huge problem. One merely has to look around and see money has been wasted, governments have been living beyond their means and no one seems willing to take charge to correct the problems.

All humans have had difficulty living within their own means and our governments have shown us how to over spend and not tighten our belts.

Each human must take responsibility for their own finances, but our governments have a simple solution lying in the palms of their hands.

If every person who insists on texting and talking on their cell phones while driving were fined fifty dollars every time they did this, imagine how much money would be deposited in the government coffers. It would not take long for budget deficits to be eliminated.

It would also cut down on traffic accidents and fatalities. My human lost a dear friend because she was killed by someone who was busy texting. Like what is more important than a human life?

And, those people are also endangering the lives of the dogs who love to ride in cars with their humans. I have not seen the statistics on how many dogs have lost their lives because someone was texting or talking on the phone about something that surely could have waited until a more convenient time.

Humans think that because all this new technology is available to them, they are entitled to use it any time they please without regard to other human's rights to stay alive.

Another means of bolstering the government coffers would be to fine all those people who do not use their headlights when it's raining.

Perhaps all states do not have a law regarding this issue, but California does. If you are using your windshield wipers, you must turn on your lights. How hard is it to do that?

Humans need to quit beating up on each other. If you love someone, you need to show them. The back of one's hand across a face is not the way to show love.

Children and old folks need to be honored and taken care of. The youth of today is this world's future. Why tarnish them by showing that violence, adultery and putting oneself first all the time, is the way to success.

And, when you have success, what gives you the right to think you are above the law, above having any morals or better than everyone else?

People need to grow up and take responsibility for their own actions and be good role models for our youth.

Our seniors need to be shown more respect also. They have tried to pave the way for generations to come. They have knowledge and insights into many things which should not be shut away, but cherished and listened to.

There is a growing problem in this nation with drugs, and I don't mean the illegal ones.

We cannot watch television any more without finding out about a new drug for some new illness that has been discovered. How many people had restless leg syndrome before there was a commercial alerting us all to the problem?

There are drugs for everything imaginable and ones we don't even know about yet. You got a problem? Call your doctor and see what he/she can prescribe to help you through the day.

In fairness to the drug companies, when they do advertise their collection of drugs, they also mention side effects (at least the ones they know about).

What part of in some cases this drug may cause heart attacks, strokes or death don't you understand? The side effects sound more terminal than the conditions for which the drugs are being used.

But, the thing that irks me the most is the parade of ads we are bombarded with every day for the guy who has erectile dysfunction. The poor guy can't get it up and needs help.

Never mind he is overweight, drinks too much, has physical, mental and social problems, he can't screw anyone, not even his wife. Never mind how she feels about having sex with him anymore, he has to be ready for his "moment."

Good sex really should take more than a moment.

The funny part of these ads is the part about if the guy experiences an erection lasting more than four hours, he should call his doctor right away.

I have news for you; if the erection lasts that long, he is in trouble and quite possibly has experienced his last erection, ever.

Sex can be a beautiful and enjoyable thing, but it's not just about sex. If one nurtures their relationship with another person and is kind, thoughtful and considerate during the relationship, sex will not be a problem.

And, at some point in one's life, sex really is not the most important thing that can happen to you.

Dogs have sex also and they understand how to do it. First of all, the male cannot mate with the female until SHE is ready. It is her call, not his.

Once the sex begins, the female locks the male in and he cannot leave until SHE is finished. What a novel idea!

Some human problems need to be left between the patient and his or her doctor. The rest of us should not have to be bombarded with insensitive commercials about how to fix someone else's problems.

Here's another solution to the economic crisis facing governments and businesses alike.

Take a look at your motor pools. How many vehicles do you have? Six, sixteen, sixty, six hundred? Vehicles are expensive items from the purchase through the use and upkeep of them. They have to be insured.

Now, take a look on any given day as to how many of those vehicles are actually in use. Three, eight, thirty, two hundred? See if you can find out if there was ever a day when all the vehicles were being used. I'll bet you can't find any days all the cars and trucks were in use.

And, to carry this even further, do all your vehicles carry painted signs as to which department they belong to? They probably do. Are all the vehicles stored in one place? Probably not.

If you cut your motor pools in half, have stick on signs showing your particular department and house these vehicles in one place, you can save millions of dollars.

So, the health department can use a car that was used the day before by the education department and fish and game can use a truck that will be used tomorrow by the parks department.

The millions that can be saved could be used to feed the hungry, find cures for diseases, solve budget deficits and find ways to have peace and goodwill on earth for all men, women and dogs.

Perhaps we need to cut back on our space exploration. I'm not saying stop it, but maybe one less adventure into space each year would provide enough funding to solve most of the difficulties we find ourselves in.

Just one more thought; how many of you are aware of how fragile our planet is? If you watch the Discovery channel, national geographic, history or science channels, you are aware of the many possibilities from within our universe that could totally destroy this planet.

Humans need to work together and enjoy whatever time nature and the universe is going to give us.

So, these are my opinions, concerns and suggestions. I have many more, but these are the ones I wanted to get off my chest. I may not be right and you may not agree with me, but to be honest, I don't care.

I have a good life; I enjoy life and I appreciate being who I am. I like being in charge and taking control of situations. Those around me have to struggle with all this and I appreciate their efforts.

If you have been reading Andrew's and my views on issues we feel are important, I'm sure you have noticed how nice and agreeable he was. I'm sure he was a sweetheart and I wish I had known him.

He found joy in everything in his life; I do too, but I'm not always as accepting as he was.

Andrew loved his mom and always referred to her as his mom. He was her first true love.

I have continued to refer to her as my human. It shows who is in charge and gives me possession over her. But, I do love her. She has been good to me and shown me things I never knew existed. Every dog should be so lucky to have a human like her.

I have been considering changing my terminology of her from my human to my mom. Well, maybe next year I will.

Breinigsville, PA USA
30 July 2010
242677BV00001B/3/P